George Albert Wentworth

Surveying and traverse table

George Albert Wentworth

Surveying and traverse table

ISBN/EAN: 9783337210366

Printed in Europe, USA, Canada, Australia, Japan

Cover: Foto ©Andreas Hilbeck / pixelio.de

More available books at **www.hansebooks.com**

SURVEYING

AND

TRAVERSE TABLE

BY

G. A. WENTWORTH, A.M.

AUTHOR OF A SERIES OF TEXT-BOOKS IN MATHEMATICS

REVISED EDITION

BOSTON, U.S.A., AND LONDON
GINN & COMPANY, PUBLISHERS
1896

TA 575
.W 47

SURVEYING.

SURVEYING.

CHAPTER I.

DEFINITIONS. INSTRUMENTS AND THEIR USES.

§ 1. Definitions.

Surveying is the art of determining and representing distances, areas, and the relative position of points upon the surface of the earth.

In plane surveying, the portion surveyed is considered as a plane.

In geodetic surveying, the curvature of the earth is regarded.

A **Plumb-Line** is a cord with a weight attached and freely suspended.

A **Vertical Line** is a line having the direction of the plumb-line.

A **Vertical Plane** is a plane embracing a vertical line.

A **Horizontal Plane** is a plane perpendicular to a vertical line.

A **Horizontal Line** is a line in a horizontal plane.

A **Horizontal Angle** is an angle the sides of which are in a horizontal plane.

A **Vertical Angle** is an angle the sides of which are in a vertical plane. If one side of a vertical angle is horizontal, and the other ascends, it is an *angle of elevation;* if one side is horizontal, and the other descends, it is an *angle of depression.*

The **Magnetic Meridian** is the direction which a bar-magnet assumes when freely supported in a horizontal position.

The **Magnetic Bearing** of a line is the angle it makes with the magnetic meridian.

Surveying commonly comprises three distinct operations; viz. :

1. The **Field Measurements,** or the process of determining by direct measurement certain lines and angles.

2. The **Computation** of the required parts from the measured lines and angles.

3. The **Plotting,** or representing on paper the measured and computed parts in relative extent and position.

THE MEASUREMENT OF LINES.

§ 2. INSTRUMENTS FOR MEASURING LINES.

The **Gunter's Chain** is generally employed in measuring land. It is 4 rods, or 66 feet, in length, and is divided into 100 links. Hence, links may be written as hundredths of a chain.

The **Engineer's Chain** is employed in surveying railroads, canals, etc. It is 100 feet long, and is divided into 100 links.

A **Tape Measure,** divided into feet and inches, is employed in measuring town-lots, cross-section work in railroad surveying, etc.

In the United States Coast and Geodetic Survey, the meter is the unit; and, when great accuracy is required, **rods** placed end to end, and brought to a horizontal position by means of a spirit-level, are employed in measuring lines.

§ 3. CHAINING.

Eleven tally-pins of iron or steel are used in chaining; also, one or more iron-shod poles called flag-staffs or range poles.

A forward chainman, or leader, and a hind chainman, or follower, are required. A flag-staff having been placed at the farther end of the line, or at some point in the line visible from the beginning, the follower takes one end of the chain, and a pin which he thrusts into the ground at the beginning of the line. The leader moves forward in the direction of the flag-staff, with the other end of the chain and the remaining ten pins, until the word "halt" from the follower warns him that he has advanced nearly the length of the chain.

At this signal he stops, and the follower, meanwhile having placed his end of the chain at the beginning of the line, directs the leader by the words "right" or "left" until the chain is exactly in line with the flag-staff. This being accomplished, and the chain stretched tightly in a horizontal position, the follower says, "down." The leader then puts in a tally-pin exactly at the end of the chain, and answers, "down"; after which the follower withdraws the pin at the beginning of the line, and the chainmen move forward until the follower nears the pin set by the leader. The follower again says, "halt," and the operation just described is repeated. This process is continued until the end of the line is reached.

If the tally-pins in the hands of the leader are exhausted before the end of the line is reached, when he has placed the last pin in the ground, he waits until the follower comes up to him. The follower gives the leader the ten pins in his hand, and records the fact that ten chains have been measured. The measuring then proceeds as before. If the distance from the last pin to the end of the line is less than a chain, the leader places his end of the chain at the end of the line, and the follower stretches tightly such a part of the chain as is necessary to reach to the last pin, and the number of links is counted. The number of whole chains is indicated by the number of pins in the hands of the follower, *the last pin remaining in the ground.*

In measuring, the chain must be held in a horizontal position. If the ground slopes, one end of the chain must be raised until the horizontal position is attained. By means of a plumb-line, or a slender staff, or, less accurately, by dropping a pin (heavy end downwards), the point vertically under the raised end of the chain may be determined. If the slope is considerable, half a chain or less may be used.

To construct a perpendicular with a chain :

1. When the point through which the perpendicular is to pass is in the line :

Let AB (Fig. 1) represent the line, and P the point. Measure from P to the right or left, $PC = 40$ links, and place a stake at C. Let one end of the chain be held at P, and the end of the eightieth link at C; then, taking the chain at the end of the thirtieth link from P, draw it so that the portions DC and DP are tightly stretched, and place a stake at D. DP will be the perpendicular required. (Why?)

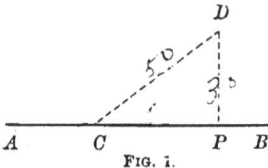

Fig. 1.

2. When the point is without the line :

Let AB (Fig. 1) be the line, and D the point. Take C any point in the line, and stretch the chain between D and C; then, let the middle of the part of the chain between C and D be held in place, and swing the end at D around until it meets the line in P. DP will be the perpendicular required. (Why?)

§ 4. Obstacles to Chaining.

1. When a tree, building, or other obstacle is encountered in measuring or extending a line, it may be passed by an offset in the following manner :

To prolong the line AB' past a building O (Fig. 2). At B erect BE perpendicular to AB; at E erect EF perpendicular to BE; at F erect $FC = BE$ perpendicular to EF: then, CD perpendicular to FC will be in the required line, and $AB + EF + CD = AD$. By constructing two other perpendiculars, $B'E'$ and $I''C'$, the accuracy of the work will be increased.

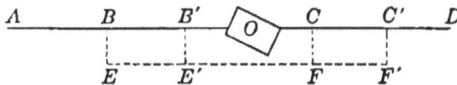

Fig. 2.

2. To measure across a body of water :

Let it be required to measure the line $ABCD$ (Fig. 3) crossing a river between B and C. Measure $BE = 400$ links ; at E erect the perpendicular $EF = 600$ links ; at B erect the perpendicular $BG = 300$ links. Place a stake at C, the intersection of AD and FG beyond the river.

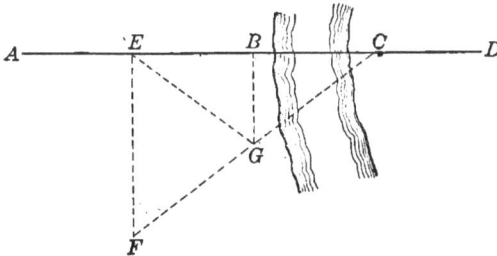

FIG. 3.

Then $BC = 400$ links. For, by similar triangles, $EF : BG :: CE : CB$. But $EF = 2\,BG$; hence, $CE = 2\,CB$, and $CB = BE = 400$ links. EG and FG should be measured, in order to test the accuracy of the work. $EG = FG = 500$ links.

Instead of the above distances, any convenient distances may be taken. For, if $EF = 2\,BG$, then $CB = BE$, and $EG = FG = \sqrt{\overline{EB}^2 + \overline{BG}^2}$.

3. To measure a line the end of which is invisible from the beginning, and intermediate points unknown :

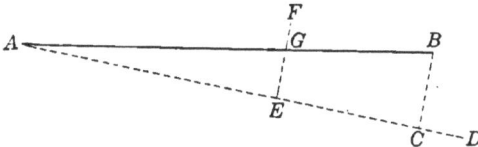

FIG. 4.

Let AB (Fig. 4) represent the line. Set up a flag-staff at D, beyond B and visible from A. From B let fall BC perpendicular to AD. Measure AC and BC. Then

$$AB = \sqrt{\overline{AC}^2 + \overline{BC}^2}.$$

To find intermediate points on AB:

At any point E on AC erect EF perpendicular to AC, and determine EG by the proportion $AC : CB :: AE : EG$. G will be a point on AB.

The line AD is called a **Random Line**.

THE MEASUREMENT OF ANGLES.

§ 5. THE SURVEYOR'S COMPASS.*

The **Surveyor's Compass** is shown on the following page.

The *compass circle* is divided into half-degrees, and is fig-
ured from 0° to 90° each way from the north and south points.
In the centre of the compass circle is the *pivot* which supports
the *magnetic needle.* The needle may be lifted from the pivot
by a spring and pressed against the glass covering of the
compass circle, when the instrument is not in use. The *main
plate* moves around the compass circle through a small arc,
read by the *vernier*, for the purpose of allowing for the variation of the needle (§ 23). The *sight standards* at the extremities of the main plate have fine slits nearly their whole length,
with circular openings at intervals; on the edges of the north
standard are *tangent scales* for reading vertical angles; and
on the outside of the south standard are two *eye-pieces* at the
same distance from the main plate as the zeros of the tangent
scales, respectively. The *telescopic sight* (a recent improvement by the Messrs. Gurley), consists of a small telescope
attached to the south standard. The main plate is furnished
with two *spirit levels* at right angles, and turns horizontally
upon the upper end of the *ball spindle*, the lower end of which
rests in a spherical socket in the top of the *tripod* or *Jacob's
staff* which supports the instrument. From the centre of the
plate at the top of the tripod a plummet is suspended by
which the centre of the compass can be placed directly over a
definite point on the ground.

*The instruments described on this and the following pages are
adjusted by the maker. If they should require re-adjustment, full
directions will be found in the manual furnished with the instruments.

The manual published by Messrs. W. & L. E. GURLEY, Troy, N. Y.,
has been freely used, by permission, in describing these instruments.

THE SURVEYOR'S COMPASS.

NOTE. The letters E and W on the face of the compass are reversed from their true positions. The reason for this is that if the sights are turned towards the west, the north end of the needle is turned towards the letter W, and if the north end of the needle is turned towards E, the sights are turned towards the east.

If the north end of the needle points exactly towards E or W, the sights will range east or west.

§ 6. USES OF THE COMPASS.

To take the bearing* of a line. Place the instrument so that the plummet will be directly over one end of the line, and level by pressing with the hands on the main plate until the bubbles are brought to the middle of the spirit levels. Turn the south end of the instrument toward you, and sight at the flag-staff at the other end of the line. Read the bearing from the north end of the needle. First, write N. or S. according as the north end of the needle is nearer N. or S. of the compass circle; secondly, write the number of degrees between the north end of the needle and the nearest zero mark; and thirdly, write E. or W. according as the north end of the needle is nearer E. or W. of the compass circle.

In Fig. 5 the bearing would be N. 45° W.

In Fig. 6 the bearing would be S. 45° W.

' In Fig. 7 the bearing would be S. 30° E.

In Fig. 8 the bearing would be N. 60° E.

If the needle coincides with the N.S. or E.W. line, the bearing would be N., S., E., or W., according as the north end of the needle is over N., S., E., or W.

As the compass circle is divided into half-degrees, the bearing may be determined pretty accurately to quarter-degrees.

When a fence or other obstruction interferes with placing the instrument over the line, it may be placed at one side, the flag-staff being placed at an equal distance from the line.

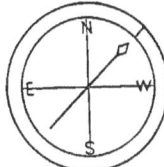

FIG. 5.

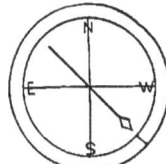

FIG. 6.

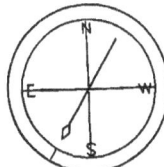

FIG. 7.

FIG. 8.

* The magnetic bearing is meant unless otherwise specified.

Local Disturbances. Before a bearing is recorded, care should be exercised that the chain, pins, and other instruments that would affect the direction of the needle, are removed from the vicinity of the compass. Even after the greatest care in this respect is exercised, the direction of the needle is often affected by iron ore, ferruginous rocks, etc.

Reverse Bearings. When the bearing of a line has been taken, the instrument should be removed to the other end of the line and the reverse bearing taken. The number of degrees should be the same as before, but the letters should be reversed.

To take the bearing of a line one end of which cannot be seen from the other. Run a random line (§ 4, 3); then (Fig. 4),

$$\tan CAB = \frac{BC}{AC};$$

whence the angle CAB may be found. This angle combined with the bearing of the random line will give the bearing required.

Another method will be given in § 19.

To measure a horizontal angle by means of the needle. Place the compass over the vertex of the angle, take the bearing of each side separately, and combine these bearings.

To measure angles of elevation. Bring the south end of the compass towards you, place the eye at the lower eye-piece, and with the hand hold a card on the front side of the north sight, so that its top edge will be at right angles to the divided edge and coincide with the zero mark; then, sighting over the top of the card, note upon a flag-staff the height cut by the line of sight; move the staff up the elevation, and carry the card along the edge of the sight until the line of sight again cuts the same height on the staff; read off the degrees of the tangent scale passed over by the card.

To measure angles of depression. Proceed in the same manner as above, using the eye-piece and tangent scale on the opposite sides of the sights, and reading from the top of the sight.

§ 7. VERNIERS.

First form. Let AB (Fig. 9) represent a portion of a rod for measuring heights (§ 32). The graduation to feet and hundredths of a foot begins at the lower end, which rests on the ground when the rod is in use. The line extending nearly across the rod at the bottom of the portion shown marks the beginning of the fourth foot. The face of the rod is divided into four columns: in the first is written the number of feet; in the second, the number of tenths; and in the third, the number of hundredths.

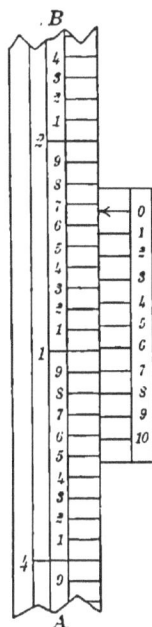

FIG. 9.

It is evident that, with the arrangement just described, heights could be measured only to hundredths of a foot. To enable us to find the height more precisely, a contrivance called a **Vernier** is used. This is shown at the right of the rod. It consists of a piece of metal or wood, the graduated part of which is $\frac{11}{100}$ of a foot in length; and this is divided into ten equal parts. Hence, one division of the vernier $= \frac{1}{10}$ of $\frac{11}{100} = \frac{11}{1000}$ of a foot; and one division of the vernier exceeds one division of the rod by $\frac{11}{1000} - \frac{1}{100} = \frac{1}{1000}$ of a foot.

The vernier slides along the face or side of the rod.

To use the vernier, place the lower end of the rod upon the ground, and move the vernier until its index or zero mark is opposite the point whose distance from the ground is desired. In the figure, the height of the index of the vernier is evidently 4.16 feet, increased by the distance of the index above the next lower line (4.16) of the rod. We shall now determine this distance.

Observe which line of the vernier is exactly opposite a line of the rod. In this case, the line of the vernier numbered 7 is opposite a line of the rod. Then, since each division of the vernier exceeds each division of the rod by $\frac{1}{1000}$ of a foot,

6 of the vernier is $\frac{1}{1000}$ of a foot above the next lower line of the rod.
5 of the vernier is $\frac{2}{1000}$ of a foot above the next lower line of the rod.
4 of the vernier is $\frac{3}{1000}$ of a foot above the next lower line of the rod.
3 of the vernier is $\frac{4}{1000}$ of a foot above the next lower line of the rod.
2 of the vernier is $\frac{5}{1000}$ of a foot above the next lower line of the rod.
1 of the vernier is $\frac{6}{1000}$ of a foot above the next lower line of the rod.
0 of the vernier is $\frac{7}{1000}$ of a foot above the next lower line of the rod.

Hence, the required reading is $4.16 + 0.007 = 4.167$ feet.

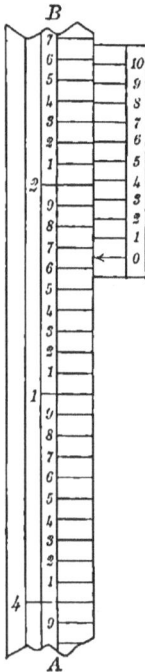

FIG. 10.

In general, the following rule is evident:

Move the vernier until its zero line is at the required height; read the height to the nearest hundredth below the index, and write in the thousandths' place the number of the division line of the vernier which stands opposite any line of the rod.

Second form. In this form (Fig. 10) the graduated part of the vernier is $\frac{9}{100}$ of a foot in length, and is divided into ten equal parts. Hence, one division of the vernier $= \frac{1}{10}$ of $\frac{9}{100} = \frac{9}{1000}$ of a foot; and one division of the vernier is less than one division of the rod by $\frac{1}{100} - \frac{9}{1000} = \frac{1}{1000}$ of a foot.

The height of the index of the vernier in Fig. 10 is 4.16 feet, increased by the distance of the index from the next lower line (4.16) of the rod. We shall now determine this distance.

We observe that the line of the vernier numbered 7 stands exactly opposite the line of the rod numbered 3. Hence,

0 of the vernier is $\frac{1}{1000}$ of a foot above the next lower line of the rod.
5 of the vernier is $\frac{2}{1000}$ of a foot above the next lower line of the rod.
4 of the vernier is $\frac{3}{1000}$ of a foot above the next lower line of the rod.
3 of the vernier is $\frac{4}{1000}$ of a foot above the next lower line of the rod.
2 of the vernier is $\frac{5}{1000}$ of a foot above the next lower line of the rod.
1 of the vernier is $\frac{6}{1000}$ of a foot above the next lower line of the rod.
0 of the vernier is $\frac{7}{1000}$ of a foot above the next lower line of the rod.

Hence, the required reading is $4.16 + 0.007 = 4.167$ feet; and the rule is evidently the same as for the first form.

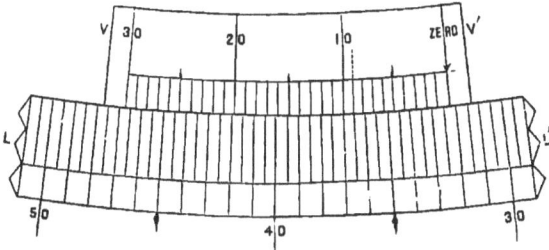

FIG. 11.

Compass Verniers. Let LL' (Fig. 11) represent the limb of the compass graduated to half-degrees, and VV' the vernier divided into thirty equal spaces, equal to twenty-nine spaces of the limb. Then one space of the vernier is less than one space of the limb by 1', and the reading may be obtained to single minutes.

In Fig. 11 the index or zero of the vernier stands between 32° and 32° 30', and the line of the vernier marked 9 coincides with a line of the limb. Hence, the reading is 32° 9'.

When the index moves from the zero line of the limb in a direction contrary to that in which the numbers of the limb run, the number of minutes obtained as above must be subtracted from 30' to obtain the minutes required.

If, however, the vernier be made double, that is, if it have thirty spaces on each side of the zero line, it is always read directly. The usual form of the double vernier, shown in Fig. 12, has only fifteen spaces on each side of the zero line. When the vernier is turned to the *right* less than 15' past a division line of the limb, read the lower figures on the *left* of the zero line at any coincidence; if moved more than 15' past a division line of the limb, read the upper figures on the *right* of the zero line at any coincidence; and *vice versa.*

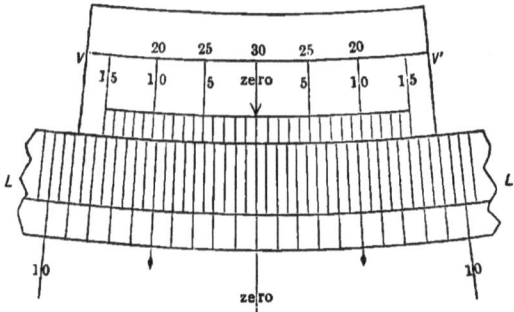

FIG. 12.

Uses of the Compass Vernier. The most important use of the vernier of the vernier compass is in setting off the variation of the needle (§ 23). If the variation of the needle at any place is known, by means of the vernier screw the compass circle may be turned through an arc equal to the variation. If the observer stands at the south end of the instrument, the vernier is turned to the right or left according as the variation is west or east. The compass will now give the bearings of the lines with the *true meridian.*

In order to retrace the lines of an old survey, turn the sights in the direction of a known line, and move the vernier until the needle indicates the old bearing. The arc moved over by the vernier will indicate the change of variation since the time of the old survey. If no line is definitely known, the *change of variation* from the time of the old survey will give the arc to be set off.

§ 8. The Surveyor's Transit.

This instrument is shown on page 209.

The *compass circle* is similar to that of the compass. The *vernier plate* which carries the *telescope* has two *verniers* and moves entirely around the *graduated limb* of the main plate. The axis of the telescope carries a *vertical circle* which measures vertical angles to single minutes by means of a vernier. Under the telescope, and attached to it, is a *spirit level* by which horizontal lines may be run, or the difference of level between two stations found. The *cross wires* are two fine fibres of spider's web, or fine platinum wires, which extend across the tube of the telescope at right angles to each other ; their intersection determines the *optical axis* or *line of collimation* of the telescope. The transit is levelled by four *levelling screws* which pass through a plate firmly fastened to the ball spindle, and rest in depressions on the upper side of the tripod plate.

A *quick centring head* enables the surveyor to change the position of the vertical axis horizontally without moving the tripod; and a *quick levelling head* enables him to bring the transit quickly to an approximately level position by the pressure of the hands, after which the levelling screws are used; also, to change the position of the transit without changing the position of the tripod legs, so as to bring the plummet exactly over any point.

To level the transit by the levelling screws. Turn the instrument until the spirit levels on the vernier plate are parallel to the vertical planes passing through opposite pairs of levelling screws. Take hold of opposite screw heads with the thumb and fore-finger of each hand, and turn both thumbs in or out as may be necessary to raise the lower side of the parallel plate and lower the other until the desired correction is made.

To use the telescope. Both the eye-piece and the object glass may be moved in and out by a rack-and-pinion movement. The eye-piece must be moved until the cross wires are perfectly distinct; then a slight movement of the eye of the observer, from side to side, will produce no apparent change in the position of the threads upon the object. The object glass must be moved until the object is distinctly visible; and this must be repeated, if the distance of the object is changed.

§ 9. USES OF THE TRANSIT.

The transit may be used for all the purposes indicated in § 6, but with much greater precision than the compass. *The principal use, however, of the transit is in measuring horizontal angles by means of the graduated limb and verniers.*

To measure a horizontal angle with the transit. Place the transit over the vertex of the angle; level, and set the limb at zero. Turn the telescope in the direction of one of the sides of the angle, clamp to the spindle; unclamp the main plate, and turn the telescope until it is in the direction of the other side of the angle, and read the angle by the verniers. The object of the two verniers on the vernier plate is to correct any mistake that might arise from the want of exact coincidence in the centres of the verniers and the limb. The correct reading may be obtained by adding to the reading of one vernier the supplement of the reading of the other, and dividing by 2.

By turning off a right angle by this method, perpendiculars may be constructed with greater facility than by the chain.

§ 10. THE THEODOLITE.

The telescope of the transit can perform a complete revolution on its axis; whence the name *transit*. The theodolite differs from the transit chiefly in that its telescope cannot be so revolved. It is not much used in this country.

§ 11. THE RAILROAD COMPASS.

This instrument has all the features of the ordinary compass, and has also a vernier plate and graduated limb for measuring horizontal angles.

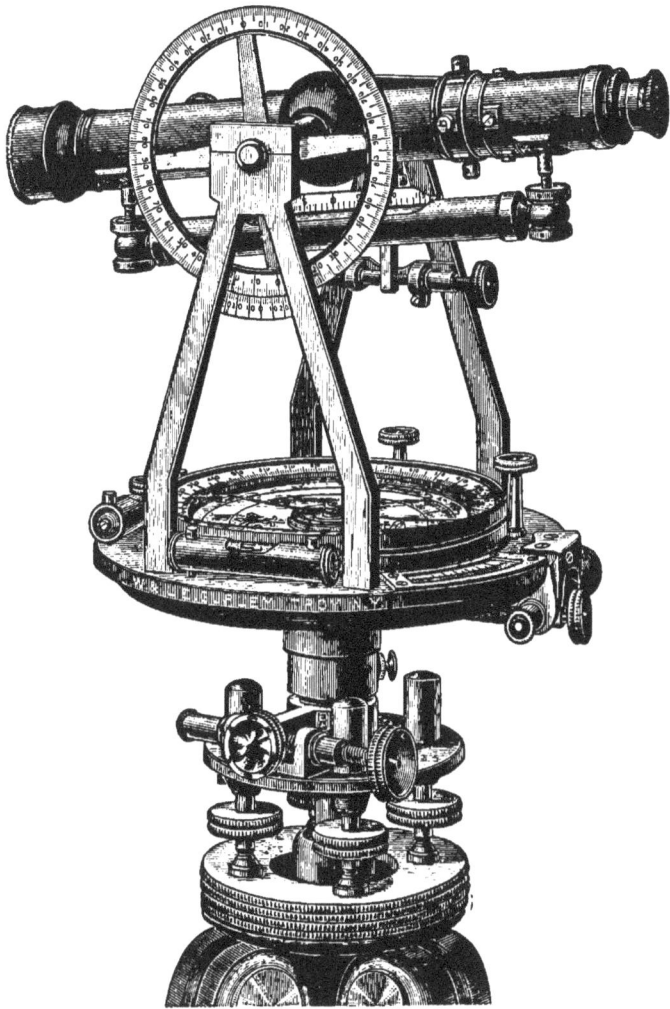

THE SURVEYOR'S TRANSIT.

§ 12. Plotting.

The principal plotting instruments are a ruler, pencil, straight-line pen, hair-spring dividers, diagonal scale, a right triangle of wood, and a circular protractor. A T-square will also be found convenient.

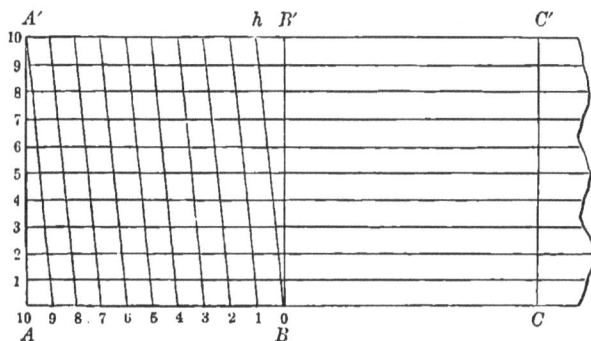

Fig. 13.

The Diagonal Scale. A portion of this scale is shown in Fig. 13. AB is the unit. AB and $A'B'$ are divided into ten equal parts, and B is joined with h, the first division point to the left of B'; the first division point to the left of B is joined with the second to the left of B', etc.

The part of the horizontal line numbered 1 intercepted between BB' and Bh is evidently $\frac{1}{10}$ of $\frac{1}{10} = \frac{1}{100}$ of the unit; the part of the horizontal line numbered 2 intercepted between BB' and Bh is $\frac{2}{100}$ of the unit, etc.

The method of using this scale is as follows :

Let it be required to lay off the distance 1.43.

Place one foot of the dividers at the intersection of the horizontal line numbered 3 and the diagonal numbered 4, and place the other foot at the intersection of the vertical line numbered 1 (CC') and the horizontal line numbered 3 ; the distance between the feet of the dividers will be the distance required. For, measuring along the horizontal line numbered 3, from CC' to BB' is 1 ; from BB' to Bh is 0.03 ; and from Bh to the diagonal numbered 4 is 0.4 ; and $1 + 0.03 + 0.4 = 1.43$.

The Circular Protractor. This instrument (Fig. 14) usually consists of a semi-circular piece of brass or german silver, having its arc divided into degrees and its centre marked.

To lay off an angle with the protractor, place the centre over the vertex of the angle, and make the diameter coincide with the given side of the angle. Mark off the number of degrees in the given angle, and draw a line through this point and the vertex.

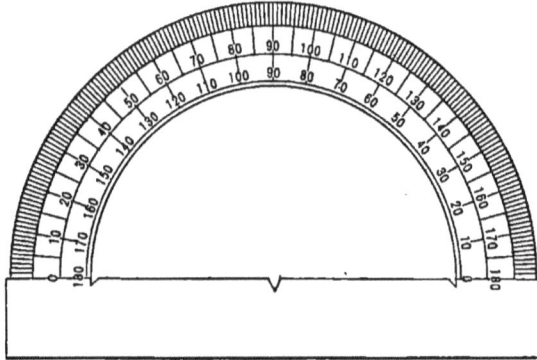

FIG. 14.

Some protractors have an arm which carries a vernier, by which angles may be constructed to single minutes.

To draw through a given point a line parallel to a given line, make one of the sides of a triangle coincide with the given line, and, placing a ruler against one of the other sides, move the triangle along the ruler until the first side passes through the given point; then draw a line along this side.

To draw through a given point a line perpendicular to a given line, make the hypotenuse of a right triangle coincide with the given line, and, placing a ruler against one of the other sides of the triangle, revolve the triangle about the vertex of the right angle as a centre until its other perpendicular side is against the ruler; then move the triangle along the ruler until the hypotenuse passes through the given point, and draw a line along the hypotenuse.

CHAPTER II.

LAND SURVEYING.

§ 13. Definition.

Land Surveying is the art of measuring, laying out, and dividing land, and preparing a plot.

§ 14. Determination of Areas.

The unit of land measure is the

$$\text{acre} = 10 \text{ square chains}$$
$$= 4 \text{ roods}$$
$$= 160 \text{ square rods, perches, or poles.}$$

Areas are referred to the horizontal plane, no allowance being made for inequalities of surface.

For convenience of reference, the following rules for areas are given:

Let A, B, and C be the angles of a triangle, and a, b, and c the opposite sides, respectively; and let $s = \frac{1}{2}(a+b+c)$.

$$\text{Area of triangle } ABC = \frac{1}{2} \text{ base} \times \text{altitude} \qquad [\text{A}]$$
$$= \frac{1}{2}bc \sin A \qquad [\text{B}]$$
$$= \frac{1}{2}\frac{a^2 \sin B \sin C}{\sin (B+C)} \qquad [\text{C}]$$
$$= \sqrt{s(s-a)(s-b)(s-c)}. \qquad [\text{D}]$$

Area of rectangle $=$ base $\times$ altitude.

Area of trapezoid $= \frac{1}{2}$ sum of parallel sides $\times$ altitude.

Problem 1. To determine the area of a triangular field.

Measure the necessary parts with a Gunter's chain, or with a chain and transit, and compute by formula [A], [B], [C], or [D].

PROBLEM 2. **To find the area of a field having any number of straight sides.**

(a) Divide the field into triangles by diagonals; find the area of each triangle and take the sum.

(b) Run a diagonal, and perpendiculars from the opposite vertices to this diagonal. The field is thus divided into right triangles, rectangles, and trapezoids, the areas of which may be found and the sum taken.

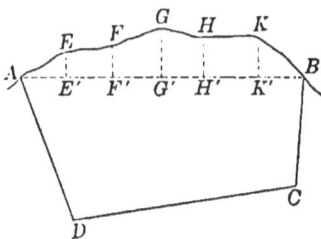
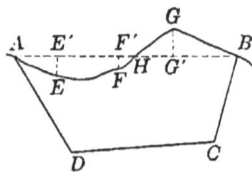

FIG. 15.   FIG. 16.

PROBLEM 3. **To find the area of a field having an irregular boundary line.**

(a) Let $AGBCD$ (Fig. 15) represent a field having a stream $AEFG \cdot HKB$ as a boundary line. Run the line AB. From E, F, G, H, and K, prominent points on the bank of the stream, let fall perpendiculars EE', FF', etc., upon AB. Regarding AE, EF, etc., as straight lines, the portion of the field cut off by AB is divided into right triangles, rectangles, and trapezoids, the necessary elements of which can be measured and the areas computed. The sum of these areas added to the area of $ABCD$ will give the area required.

(b) When the irregular boundary line crosses the straight line joining its extremities, as in Fig. 16, the areas of $AEFH$ and HGB may be found separately, as in the preceding case. Then the area required $= ABCD + HGB - AEFH$.

PROBLEM 4. **To determine the area of a field from two interior stations.**

Let $ABCD$ (Fig. 17) represent a field, and P and P' two stations within it. Measure PP' with great exactness. Measure the angles between PP' and the lines from P and P' to the corners of the field.

In the triangle $PP'D$, PP' and the angles $P'PD$ and $PP'D$ are known; hence, PD may be found. In like manner, PC may be found. Then in the triangle PDC, PD, PC, and the angle DPC are known; hence, the area of PDC may be computed.

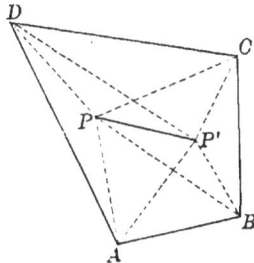

In like manner, the areas of all the triangles about P and P' may be determined.

Area $ABCD = PAD + PDC + PCB + PBA$. Also

Area $ABCD = P'AD + P'DC + P'CB + P'BA$.

FIG. 17.

PROBLEM 5. **To determine the area of a field from two exterior stations.**

Let $ABCD$ (Fig. 18) represent the field, and P and P' the stations. Determine the areas of the triangles PAD, PDC, PCB, and PBA, as in the preceding problem.

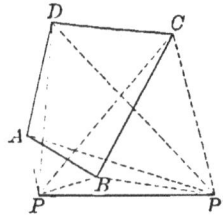

Area $ABCD = PAD + PDC + PBC - PBA$. Also,

Area $ABCD = P'AD + P'DC + P'BA - P'BC$.

FIG. 18.

EXERCISE I.

1. Required the area of a triangular field whose sides are respectively 13, 14, and 15 chains.

2. Required the area of a triangular field whose sides are respectively 20, 30, and 40 chains.

3. Required the area of a triangular field whose base is 12.60 chains, and altitude 6.40 chains.

4. Required the area of a triangular field which has two sides 4.50 and 3.70 chains, respectively, and the included angle 60°.

5. Required the area of a field in the form of a trapezium, one of whose diagonals is 9 chains, and the two perpendiculars upon this diagonal from the opposite vertices 4.50 and 3.25 chains.

6. Required the area of the field $ABCDEF$ (Fig. 19), if
$AE = 9.25$ chains, $FF' = 6.40$ chains, $BE = 13.75$ chains, DD'
= 7 chains, $DB = 10$ chains, $CC' =$
4 chains, and $AA' = 4.75$ chains.

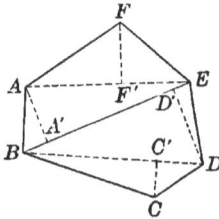

FIG. 19.

7. Required the area of the field
$ABCDEF$ (Fig. 20), if
$AF' =$ 4 chains, $FF' =$ 6 chains,
$EE' = 6.50$ chains, $AE' =$ 9 chains,
$AD =$ 14 chains, $AC' = 10$ chains,
$AB' = 6.50$ chains, $BB' =$ 7 chains,
$CC' = 6.75$ chains.

8. Required the area of the field $AGBCD$ (Fig. 15), if the
diagonal $AC = 5$, BB' (the perpen-
dicular from B to AC) = 1, DD' (the
perpendicular from D to AC) = 1.60,
$EE' = 0.25$, $FF' = 0.25$, $GG' = 0.60$,
$HH' = 0.52$, $KK' = 0.54$, $AE' = 0.2$,
$E'F' = 0.50$, $F'G' = 0.45$, $G'H' =$
0.45, $H'K' = 0.60$, and $K'B = 0.40$.

9. Required the area of the field
$AGBCD$ (Fig. 16), if $AD = 3$, AC

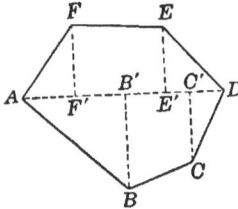

FIG. 20.

= 5, $AB = 6$, angle $DAC = 45°$, angle $BAC = 30°$, $AE' =$
0.75, $AF' = 2.25$, $AH = 2.53$, $AG' = 3.15$, $EE' = 0.60$, $FF' =$
0.40, and $GG' = 0.75$.

10. Determine the area of the field $ABCD$ from two interior
stations, P and P', if $PP' = 1.50$ chains,

$PP'C =$ 89° 35', $PP'D = 349° 45'$, $P'PD = 165° 40'$,
$PP'B = 185° 30'$, $P'PB =$ 3° 35', $P'PC = 303° 15'$.
$PP'A = 309° 15'$, $P'PA = 113° 45'$,

11. Determine the area of the field $ABCD$ from two exterior
stations, P and P', if $PP' = 1.50$ chains,

$P'PB =$ 41° 10', $P'PD = 104° 45'$, $PP'B = 132° 15'$,
$P'PA =$ 55° 45', $PP'D =$ 66° 45', $PP'A = 103°$ 0'.
$P'PC =$ 77° 20', $PP'C =$ 95° 40',

RECTANGULAR SURVEYING.

§ 15. DEFINITIONS.

An **East and West Line** is a line perpendicular to the magnetic meridian.

The **Latitude of a line** is the distance between the east and west lines through its extremities.

The **Departure of a line** is the distance between the meridians through its extremities.

NOTE. When a line extends north of the initial point the latitude is called a northing; when it extends south, a southing; when it extends east the departure is called an easting; when it extends west, a westing.

The **Meridian Distance of a point** is its distance from a meridian.

The **Double Meridian Distance of a course** is double the distance of the middle point of the course from the meridian.

Let AB (Fig. 21) represent a line, and NAS the magnetic meridian. Let BB' be perpendicular to NS.

The bearing of the line AB is the angle BAB'.

The latitude of the line AB is AB'.

The departure of the line AB is BB'.

The meridian distance of the point B is BB'.

In the right triangle ABB',

$$AB' = AB \times \cos BAB',$$

and $$BB' = AB \times \sin BAB'.$$

Hence, *latitude* $= distance \times cos\ of\ bearing,$

and *departure* $= distance \times sin\ of\ bearing.$

The latitudes and departures corresponding to any distance and bearing may be found from the above formulas by means of a table of natural sines and cosines, or from "The Traverse Table."*

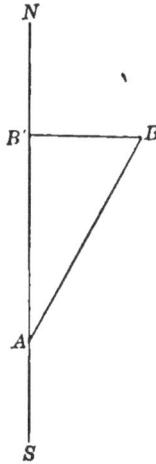

FIG. 21.

* See Table VII. of Wentworth & Hill's Five-Place Logarithmic and Trigonometric Tables.

§ 16. Field Notes, Computation, and Plotting.

The field notes are kept in a book provided for the purpose.
The page is ruled in three columns, in the first of which is
written the number of the station; in the second, the bearing
of the side; and in the third, the length of the side.

Example 1. To survey the field *ABCD* (Fig. 22).

FIELD NOTES.

1	N. 20° E.	8.66
2	S. 70° E.	5.00
3	S. 10° E.	10.00
4	N. 70° W.	10.00

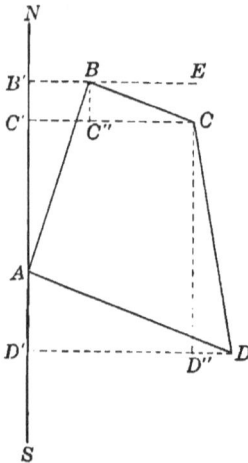

FIG. 22.

(a) To obtain the field notes.

Place the compass at *A*, the first station,
and take the bearing of *AB* (§ 6); suppose
it to be N. 20° E. Write the result in the
second column of the field notes opposite
the number of the station. Measure *AB*
= 8.66 chains, and write the result in the
third column of the field notes.

Place the compass at *B*, and, after testing
the bearing of *AB* (§ 6), take the bearing of
BC, measure *BC*, and write the results in the
field notes; and so continue until the bearing
and length of each side have been recorded.

(b) To compute the area.

I.	II.	III.	IV.	V.	VI.	VII.	VIII.	IX.	X.	XI.
Side.	Bearing.	Dist.	N.	S.	E.	W.	M.D.	D.M.D.	N.A.	S.A.
AB	N. 20° E.	8.66	AB' 8.14	....	BB' 2.96	...	BB' 2.96	BB' 2.96	2ABB' 24.0944	....
BC	S. 70° E.	5.00	....	B'C' 1.71	C"C 4.70	...	CC' 7.66	BB'+CC' 10.62	....	2C'CBB' 18.1802
CD	S. 10° E.	10.00	....	C'D' 9.85	D"D 1.74	...	DD' 9.40	CC'+DD' 17.06	....	2D'DCC' 168.0410
DA	N. 70° W.	10.00	D'A 3.42	....	....	DD' 9.40	0	DD' 9.40	2ADD' 32.1480	....
			33.66	11.56	11.56	9.40	9.40			56.2424	186.2012

The survey may begin at any corner of the field ; but in computing the area, the field notes should be arranged so that the most eastern or most western station will stand first. For the sake of uniformity, we shall always begin with the most *western* station, and keep the field on the *right* in passing around it.

$$\begin{array}{r} 186.2012 \\ 56.2424 \\ \hline 2 \boxed{\,129.9588\,} \\ 10 \boxed{\,64.98\,} \text{ sq. ch.} \\ 6.498 \text{ acres.} \end{array}$$

The field notes occupy the first three of the eleven columns in the above tablet. Columns IV., V., VI., and VII. contain the latitudes and departures corresponding to the sides, and taken from the Traverse Table. The lines represented by these numbers are indicated immediately above each number. Column VIII. contains the meridian distances of the points B, C, D, and A, taken in order. Column IX. contains the double meridian distances of the courses. Their composition is indicated by the letters immediately above the numbers. Column X. contains the products of the double meridian distances by the northings in the same line. The first number,

$$24.0944 = 2.96 \times 8.14 = BB' \times AB' = 2 \text{ area of the triangle } ABB';$$
$$32.1480 = 9.40 \times 3.42 = DD' \times AD' = 2 \text{ area of the triangle } ADD'.$$

Column XI. contains the products of the double meridian distances by the southings in the same line. The first number,

$$18.1602 = 10.62 \times 1.71 = (BB' + CC') \times B'C'$$
$$= 2 \text{ area of the trapezoid } C'CBB';$$
$$168.0410 = 17.06 \times 9.85 = (CC' + DD') \times D'C'$$
$$= 2 \text{ area of the trapezoid } D'DCC'.$$

The sum of the north areas in column X.
$$= 56.2424 = 2 (ABB' + ADD').$$

The sum of the south areas in column XI.
$$= 186.2012 = 2 (C'CBB' + D'DCC').$$

But $\qquad (C'CBB' + D'DCC') - (ABB' + ADD') = ABCD.$

Hence, $\qquad 2(C'CBB' + D'DCC') - 2(ABB' + ADD') = 2ABCD;$

that is, $186.2012 - 56.2424 = 129.9588 = 2 ABCD.$

Hence, area $ABCD = \frac{1}{2}$ of $129.9588 = 64.9794$ sq. ch. $= 6.498$ acres.

(c) To make the plot.

The plot or map may be drawn to any desired scale. If a line one inch in length in the plot represents a line one chain in length, the plot is said to be drawn to a scale of one chain to an inch. In this case the plot (Fig. 22) is drawn to a scale of eight chains to an inch.

Draw the line NAS to represent the magnetic meridian, and lay off the first northing $AB' = 8.14$ (§ 12). Draw the indefinite line $B'E$ perpendicular to NS and lay off $B'B$, the first easting = 2.96. Join A and B; then the line AB will represent the first side of the field. Through B draw BC'' perpendicular to BB', and make $BC'' = 1.71$, the first southing. Through C'' draw $C''C$ perpendicular to BC'', and equal to 4.70, the second easting. Join B and C. The line BC will represent the second side of the field.

Proceed in like manner until the field is completely represented. The extremity of the last line $D'A$, measured from D', should fall at A. This will be a test of the accuracy of the plot.

By drawing the diagonal AC, and letting fall upon it perpendiculars from B and D, the quadrilateral $ABCD$ is divided into two triangles, the bases and altitudes of which may be measured and the area computed approximately.

Other methods of plotting will suggest themselves, but the method just explained is one of the best.

Balancing the Work.

In the survey, we pass entirely around the field; hence, we move just as far north as south. Therefore, the sum of the northings should equal the sum of the southings. In like manner, the sum of the eastings should equal the sum of the westings. In this way the accuracy of the field work may be tested.

In Example 1, the sum of the northings is equal to the sum of the southings, being 11.56 in each case; and the sum of the eastings is equal to the sum of the westings, being 9.40 in each case. Hence, the work balances.

In actual practice the work seldom balances. When it does not balance, corrections are generally applied to the latitudes and departures, by the following rules :

The perimeter of the field : any one side

:: total error in latitude   : correction ;

:: total error in departure : correction.

If special difficulty has been experienced in taking a particular bearing, or in measuring a particular line, the corrections should be applied to the corresponding latitudes and departures.

The amount of error allowable varies in the practice of different surveyors, and according to the nature of the ground. An error of 1 link in 8 chains would not be considered too great on smooth, level ground; while, on rough ground, an error of 1 link in 2 or 3 chains might be allowed. If the error is considerable, the field measurements should be repeated.

EXAMPLE 2. Let it be required to survey the field *AB CDEF* (Fig. 23).

FIELD NOTES.

1	N. 73° 30′ W.	5.00
2	S. 16° 30′ W.	5.00
3	N. 28° 30′ W.	7.07
4	N. 20° 00′ E.	11.18
5	S. 43° 30′ E.	5.00
6	S. 13° 30′ E.	10.00

```
      243.0888
       81.4955
   2 | 161.5933
  10 |  80.7967
        8.0797  acres.
```

EXPLANATION. The first station in the field notes is *D*, but we rearrange the numbers in the tablet so that *A* stands first. The northings and southings balance, but the eastings exceed the westings by 1 link. We apply the correction to the westing 4.79 (the distance *DE* being in doubt), making it 4.80, and rewrite all the latitudes and departures in the next four columns, incorporating the correction. In practice, the corrected numbers are written in red ink.

43.25 : 5 :: 0.01 : x.

Side	Bearing	Dist.	N.	S.	E.	W.	N′.	S′.	E′.	W′.	M. D.	D. M. D.	N. A.	S. A.
FA	N.28°30′W.	7.07	6.21			3.37	F′A 6.21			F′F 3.37	0	E′E+F′F 8.16	2 AFF′ 20.9277	
EF	S.16°30′W.	5.00		4.79		1.42		E′F′ 4.79		1.42	F′F 3.37	D′D+E′E 14.38		2 F′FEE′ 39.0864
DE	N.73°30′W.	5.00	1.42			4.79	D′E′ 1.42			E′E 4.80	E′E 4.79	D′D+E′E 14.38	2 D′DEE′ 20.4196	
CD	S.13°30′E.	10.00		9.72	2.33			C′D′ 9.72	D′D 2.33		D′D 9.59	C′C+D′D 16.85		2 D′DCC′ 163.7820
BC	S.43°30′E.	5.00		3.63	3.44			B′C 3.63	C′C 3.44		C′C 7.26	C′C+D′D 11.08		2 C′CB′D′ 40.2204
AB	N.20°00′E.	11.18	10.51		3.82		A′B′ 10.51		B′B 3.82		B′B 3.82	B′B 3.82	2 ABB′ 40.1482	
Totals		43.25	18.14	18.14	9.59	9.58							81.4955	243.0888

The remainder of the computation does not require explanation.

It will be seen that this method of computing areas is perfectly general.

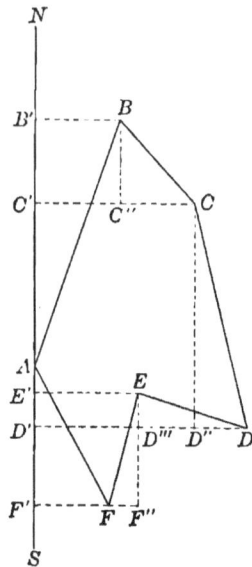

Fig. 23.

§ 17. Supplying Omissions.

If, for any reason, the bearing and length of any side do not appear in the field notes, the latitude and departure of this side may be found in the following manner:

Find the latitudes and departures of the other sides as usual. The difference between the northings and southings will give the northing or southing of the unknown side, and the difference between the eastings and westings will give the easting or westing of the unknown side.

If the length and bearing of the unknown side are desired, they may be found by solving the right triangle, whose sides are the latitude and departure found by the method just explained, and whose hypotenuse is the length required.

§ 18. Irregular Boundaries.

If a field have irregular boundaries, its area may be found by offsets, as explained in § 14, Prob. 3.

§ 19. Obstructions.

If the end of a line be not visible from its beginning, or if the line be inaccessible, its length and bearing may be found as follows:

1. By means of a random line (§ 4, 3).

2. When it is impossible to run a random line, which is frequently the case on account of the extent of the obstruction, the following method may be used:

Let AB (Fig. 24) represent an inaccessible line whose extremities A and B only are known, and B invisible from A.

Set flag-staffs at convenient points, C and D. Find the bearings and lengths of AC, CD, and DB, and then proceed to find the latitude and departure of AB, as in § 17.

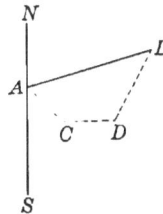

FIG. 24.

EXAMPLE. Suppose that we have the following notes (see Fig. 24):

SIDE.	BEARING.	DIST.	N.	S.	E.	W.
AC	S. 45° E.	3.00		2.12	2.12	
CD	E.	3.50			3.50	
DB	N. 30° E.	4.83	4.18		2.42	
			4.18	2.12	8.04	0

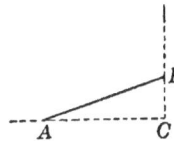

FIG. 25.

4.18
2.12
2.06

The northing of AB is 2.06, and the easting, 8.04; which numbers may be entered in the tablet in the columns N. and E., opposite the side AB.

If the bearing and length of AB are required, construct the right triangle ABC (Fig. 25), making $AC = 8.04$ and $BC = 2.06$.

$$\tan BAC = \frac{BC}{AC} = \frac{2.06}{8.04} = 0.256.$$

Hence, the angle $BAC = 14° 22'$.

Also, $AB = \sqrt{\overline{AC^2} + \overline{BC^2}} = \sqrt{8.04^2 + 2.06^2} = 8.29$.

Therefore, the bearing and length of AB are N. 75° 38' E. and 8.29.

NOTE. Keep all the decimal figures until the result is obtained; then reject all decimal figures but two, increasing the last decimal figure retained by 1, if the third decimal figure is 5 or greater than 5.

EXERCISE II.

In examples 5 and 6 detours were made on account of inaccessible sides (§ 19, 2). The notes of the detours are written in braces.

1.

Sta.	Bearings.	Dist.
1	S. 75° E.	6.00
2	S. 15° E.	4.00
3	S. 75° W.	6.93
4	N. 45° E.	5.00
5	N. 45° W.	5.19½

2.

Sta.	Bearings.	Dist.
1	N. 45° E.	10.00
2	S. 75° E.	11.55
3	S. 15° W.	18.21
4	N. 45° W.	19.11

3.

Sta.	Bearings.	Dist.
1	N. 15° E.	3.00
2	N. 75° E.	6.00
3	S. 15° W.	6.00
4	N. 75° W.	5.20

4.

Sta.	Bearings.	Dist.
1	N. 89°45' E.	4.94
2	S. 7°00' W.	2.30
3	S. 23°00' E.	1.52
4	S. 0°15' E.	2.57
5	N. 84°45' W.	5.11
6	N. 2°30' W.	5.79

5.

Sta.	Bearings.	Dist.
1	S. 2°15' E.	9.68
2 {	N. 51°45' W.	2.39
	S. 85°00' W.	6.47
	S. 55°10' W.	1.62
3	N. 3°45' E.	6.39
4	S. 66°45' E.	1.70
5	N. 15°00' E.	4.98
6	S. 82°45' E.	6.03

6.

Sta.	Bearings.	Dist.
1 {	S. 81°20' W.	4.28
	N. 76°30' W.	2.67
2	N. 5°00' E.	8.68
3	S. 87°30' E.	5.54
4 {	S. 7°00' E.	1.79
	S. 27°00' E.	1.94
	S. 10°30' E.	5.35
	N. 76°45' W.	1.70

7.

Sta.	Bearings.	Dist.
1	N. 6°15' W.	6.31
2	S. 81°50' W.	4.06
3	S. 5°00' E.	5.86
4	N. 88°30' E.	4.12

8.

Sta.	Bearings.	Dist.
1	N. 5°30' W.	6.08
2	S. 82°30' W.	6.51
3	S. 3°00' E.	5.33
4	E.	6.72

9.

Sta.	Bearings.	Dist.
1	N. 20°00' E.	4.62½
2	N. 73°00' E.	4.16½
3	S. 45°15' E.	6.18½
4	S. 38°30' W.	8.00
5	Wanting.	Wanting.

10.

Sta.	Bearings.	Dist.
1	S. 3°00' E.	4.23
2	S. 86°45' W.	4.78
3	S. 37°00' W.	2.00
4	N. 81°00' W.	7.45
5	N. 61°00' W.	2.17
6	N. 32°00' E.	8.68
7	S. 75°50' E.	6.38
8	S. 14°45' W.	0.98
9	S. 79°15' E.	4.52

§ 20. Modification of the Rectangular Method.

The area of a field may be found by a modification of the rectangular method, if its sides and interior angles are known.

Let A, B, C, D, represent the interior angles of the field $ABCD$ (Fig. 26). Let the side AB determine the direction of reference.

The bearing of AB, with reference to AB, is $0°$.

The bearing of BC, with reference to AB, is the angle $b = 180° - B$.

The bearing of CD, with reference to AB, is the angle $c = C - b$.

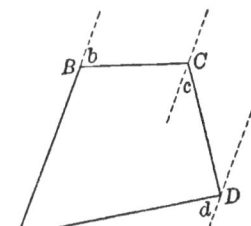
Fig. 26.

The bearing of DA, with reference to AB, is the angle $d = A$.

The area may now be computed by the rectangular method, regarding AB as the magnetic meridian.

In practice, the exterior angles, when acute, are usually measured.

As the interior angles may be measured with considerable accuracy by the transit, the latitudes and departures should be obtained by using a table of natural sines and cosines.

Exercise III.

1. Find the area of the field $ABCD$, in which the angle $A = 120°$, $B = 60°$, $C = 150°$, and $D = 30°$; and the side $AB = 4$ chains, $BC = 4$ chains, $CD = 6.928$ chains, and $DA = 8$ chains.

Keep three decimal places, and use the Traverse Table.

2. Find the area of the farm $ABCDE$, in which the angle $A = 106° 19'$, $B = 99° 40'$, $C = 120° 20'$, $D = 86° 8'$, and $E = 127° 33'$; and the side $AB = 79.86$ rods, $BC = 121.13$ rods, $CD = 90$ rods, $DE = 100.65$ rods, and $EA = 100$ rods.

Use the table of natural sines and cosines, keeping two decimal places as usual.

§ 21. GENERAL REMARKS ON DETERMINING AREAS.

Operations depending upon the reading of the magnetic needle must lack accuracy. Hence,' when great accuracy is required (which is seldom the case in land surveying), the rectangular method (§§ 16–19) cannot be employed.

The best results are obtained by the methods explained in §§ 14 and 20, the horizontal angles being measured with the transit, and great care exercised in measuring the lines.

§ 22. THE VARIATION OF THE NEEDLE.

The **Magnetic Declination**, or variation of the needle, at any place, is the angle which the magnetic meridian makes with the true meridian, or north and south line. The variation is east or west, according as the north end of the needle lies east or west of the true meridian. Western variation is indicated by the sign +, and eastern by the sign −.

Irregular Variations are sudden deflections of the needle, which occur without apparent cause. They are sometimes accompanied by auroral displays and thunder storms, and are most frequent in years of greatest sun-spot activity.

Solar-Diurnal Variation. North of the equator, the north end of the needle moves to the west, from 8 A.M. to 1.30 P.M., about 6' in winter and 11' in summer, and then returns gradually to its normal position.

Secular Variation is a change in the same direction for about a century and a half; then in the opposite direction for about the same time.

The line of no variation, or the **Agonic Line**, is a line joining those places at which the magnetic meridian coincides with the true meridian. In the United States, this line at present (1895) passes through Michigan, Ohio, Eastern Kentucky, the extreme southwest of Virginia, and the Carolinas. It is moving gradually westward, so that the variation is increasing at places east of this line, and decreasing at places west of this line. East of this line the variation is westerly, and west of this line the variation is easterly.

The table on pages 234 and 235, which has been prepared by permission from data furnished by the United States Coast and Geodetic Survey, shows the magnetic variation at different places in the United States and Canada for several years; also, the annual change for 1895.

§ 23. To Establish a True Meridian.

This may be done as follows:

1. *By means of Burt's Solar Compass* (§ 25).
2. *By observations of Polaris.*

The North Star or Polaris revolves about the pole at present at the distance of about $1\frac{1}{4}°$; hence, it is on the meridian twice in 23 h. 56 m. 4 s. (a sidereal day), once above the pole, called the upper culmination, and 11 h. 58 m. 2 s. later below the pole, called the lower culmination. It attains its greatest eastern or western elongation, or greatest distance from the meridian, 5 h. 59 m. 1 s. after the culmination.

The following table gives the mean local time of the upper culmination of Polaris for 1895 at Washington. The time is growing later at the rate of about one minute in three years.

MONTH.	FIRST DAY.	ELEVENTH DAY.	TWENTY-FIRST DAY.
	H. M.	*H. M.*	*H. M.*
January . . .	6 35 P.M.	5 55 P.M.	5 16 P.M.
February . .	4 32 P.M.	3 53 P.M.	3 14 P.M.
March	2 42 P.M.	2 03 P.M.	1 23 P.M.
April	12 40 P.M.	12 00 M.	11 17 A.M.
May	10 38 A.M.	9 59 A.M.	9 20 A.M.
June	8 37 A.M.	7 57 A.M.	7 18 A.M.
July	6 39 A.M.	6 00 A.M.	5 21 A.M.
August	4 38 A.M.	4 00 A.M.	3 19 A.M.
September . .	2 36 A.M.	1 57 A.M.	1 18 A.M.
October . . .	12 39 A.M.	11 59 P.M.	11 20 P.M.
November . .	10 37 P.M.	9 57 P.M.	9 18 P.M.
December . .	8 39 P.M.	7 59 P.M.	7 20 P.M.

The time of the upper culmination of Polaris may be found by means of the star Mizar, which is the middle one of the three stars in the handle of the Dipper (in the constellation of the Great Bear). It crosses the meridian at almost exactly the same time as Polaris. Suspend from a height of about 20 feet a plumb-line, placing the bob in a pail of water to lessen its vibrations. About 15 feet south of the plumb-line, upon a horizontal board firmly supported at a convenient height, place a compass sight fastened to a board a few inches square. At night, when Mizar by estimation approaches the meridian, place the compass sight in line with Polaris and the plumb-line, and move it so as to keep it in this line until the plumb-line also falls on Mizar (Fig. 27). Note the time; then (1895) fifty-one seconds later Polaris will be on the meridian.

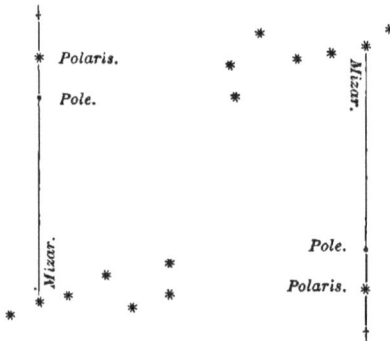

FIG. 27.

This interval is gradually increasing at the rate of 21 seconds a year.

If the lower culmination takes place at night, the time may be found in a similar manner.

When Mizar cannot conveniently be used, as in the spring, δ Cassiopeiae may be employed. This is the star at the bottom of the first stroke of the W frequently imagined to connect roughly the five brightest stars in Cassiopeia. In 1895 it culminates 1.75 minutes before Polaris, with an annual increase of the interval of 20 seconds.

Instead of the compass sight, any upright with a small opening or slit may be used.

(*a*) **To locate the true meridian by the position of Polaris at its culmination.**

1. *By using the apparatus described in finding the time of culmination.* At the time of culmination bring Polaris, the plumb-line, and the compass sight into line. The compass sight and the plumb-line will give two points in the true meridian.

2. *By means of the transit.* Bring the telescope to bear on Polaris at the time of culmination, holding a light near to make the wires visible, if the observation is made at night. The telescope will then lie in the plane of the meridian, which may be marked by bringing the telescope to a horizontal position.

(*b*) **To locate the meridian by the position of Polaris at greatest elongation.**

The **Azimuth** of a star is the angle which the meridian plane makes with a vertical plane passing through the star and the zenith of the observer.

A star is said to be at its **greatest elongation,** when its vertical circle ZN (Fig. 28) is tangent to its diurnal circle, that is, perpendicular to the hour circle PN.

Let Z (Fig. 28) represent the zenith of the place, P the pole, and N Polaris at its greatest elongation; that is, when its vertical circle ZN is perpendicular to the hour circle PN. Let ZP, ZN, and PN be arcs of great circles; then N will be a right angle.

$$\sin PN = \cos (90° - ZP) \cos (90° - Z).$$
$$\text{[Spher. Trig. § 47.]}$$

But $ZP =$ the complement of the latitude.

Hence, $90° - ZP =$ the latitude of the place.

Hence, $\sin PN = \cos \text{latitude} \times \sin Z.$

Hence, $\sin Z = \dfrac{\sin PN}{\cos \text{latitude}}.$

FIG. 28.

Hence, Z (the azimuth of Polaris) can be found if the latitude of the place and the greatest elongation of Polaris (PN) are known.

The following table gives the mean value of the latter element for each year from 1895 to 1906.

GREATEST ELONGATION OF POLARIS.

1895	1° 15.1′	1899	1° 13.8′	1903	1° 12.6′
1896	1° 14.8′	1900	1° 13.5′	1904	1° 12.3′
1897	1° 14.5′	1901	1° 13.2′	1905	1° 12.0′
1898	1° 14.1′	1902	1° 12.9′	1906	1° 11.7′

The greatest elongation of Polaris, or the polar distance, is given in the Nautical Almanac. The table gives this element for Jan. 1. It may be found for other dates by interpolation.

To obtain a line in the direction of Polaris at greatest elongation.

1. *By using the apparatus for finding the time of culmination.* A few minutes before the time of greatest elongation (5 h. 59 m. 1 s. after culmination), place the compass sight in line with the plumb-line and Polaris, and keep it in line with these, by moving the board in the opposite direction, until the star begins to recede. At this moment the sight and plumb-line are in the required line.

2. *By means of the transit.* A few minutes before the time of greatest elongation, bring the telescope to bear on the star, and follow it, keeping the vertical wire over the star until it begins to recede. The telescope will then be in the required line.

To establish the meridian. Having the transit sighted in the direction of the line just found, turn it through an angle equal to the azimuth in the proper direction.

§ 24. DIVIDING LAND.

The surveyor must, for the most part, depend on his general knowledge of Geometry and Trigonometry, and his own ingenuity, for the solutions of problems that arise in dividing land.

PROBLEM 1. **To divide a triangular field into two parts having a given ratio, by a line through a given vertex.**

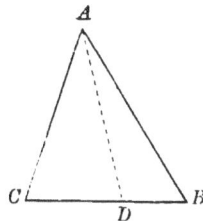

Let ABC (Fig. 29) be the triangle, and A the given vertex.

Divide BC at D, so that $\dfrac{BD}{DC}$ equals the given ratio, and join A and D. ABD and ADC will be the parts required; for

$$ABD : ADC :: BD : DC.$$

FIG. 29.

PROBLEM 2. **To cut off from a triangular field a given area, by a line parallel to the base.**

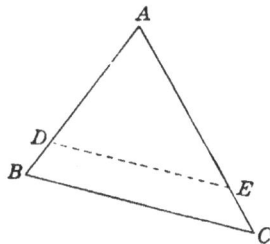

Let ABC (Fig. 30) be the triangle, and let DE be the division line required.

$$\sqrt{ABC} : \sqrt{ADE} :: AB : AD.$$

$$\therefore AD = AB \sqrt{\frac{ADE}{ABC}}.$$

FIG. 30.

PROBLEM 3. **To divide a field into two parts having a given ratio, by a line through a given point in the perimeter.**

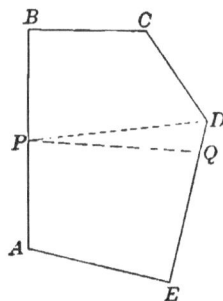

Let $ABCDE$ (Fig. 31) represent the field, P the given point, and PQ the required division line.

The areas of the whole field and of the required parts having been determined, run the line PD from P to a corner D, dividing the field, as near as possible, as required. Determine the area $PBCD$.

FIG. 31.

The triangle PDQ represents the part which must be added to $PBCD$ to make the required division.

$$\text{Area } PDQ = \tfrac{1}{2} \times PD \times DQ \times \sin PDQ.$$

$$\text{Hence, } DQ = \frac{2 \text{ area } PDQ}{PD \times \sin PDQ}.$$

NOTE. $DQ = \dfrac{2 \text{ area } PDQ}{\text{perpendicular from } P \text{ on } DE}.$ This perpendicular from P on DE may be run and measured directly.

PROBLEM 4. **To divide a field into a given number of parts, so that access to a pond of water is given to each.**

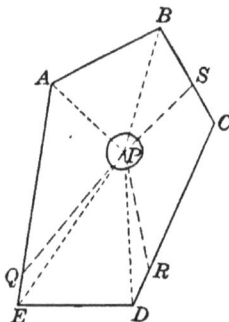

FIG. 32.

Let $ABCDE$ (Fig. 32) represent the field, and P the pond. Let it be required to divide the field into four parts. Find the area of the field and of each part.

Let AP be one division line. Run PE, and find the area APE. Take the difference between APE and the area of one of the required parts; this will give the area of the triangle PQE, from which QE may be found, as in Problem 3. Join P and Q; PAQ will be one of the required parts. In like manner, PQR and PAS are determined; whence, PSR must be the fourth part required.

EXERCISE IV.

1. From the square $ABCD$, containing 6 A. 1 R. 24 P., part off 3 A. by a line EF parallel to AB.

2. From the rectangle $ABCD$, containing 8 A. 1 R. 24 P., part off 2 A. 1 R. 32 P. by a line EF parallel to $AD = 7$ ch. Then, from the remainder of the rectangle, part off 2 A. 3 R. 25 P., by a line GH parallel to EB.

3. Part off 6 A. 3 R. 12 P. from a rectangle $ABCD$, containing 15 A., by a line EF parallel to AB; AD being 10 ch.

4. From a square $ABCD$, whose side is 9 ch., part off a triangle which shall contain 2 A. 1 R. 36 P., by a line BE drawn from B to the side AD.

5. From *ABCD*, representing a rectangle, whose length is 12.65 ch., and breadth 7.58 ch., part off a trapezoid which shall contain 7 A. 3 R. 24 P., by a line *BE* from *B* to *DC*.

6. In the triangle *ABC*, *AB* =12 ch., *AC* =10 ch., *BC* =8 ch.; part off 1 A. 2 R. 16 P., below the line *DE* parallel to *AB*.

7. In the triangle *ABC*, *AB* = 26 ch., *AC* = 20 ch., and *BC* = 16 ch.; part off 6 A. 1 R. 24 P., below the line *DE* parallel to *AB*.

8. It is required to divide the triangular field *ABC* among three persons whose claims are as the numbers 2, 3, and 5, so that they may all have the use of a watering-place at *C*; *AB* = 10 ch., *AC* = 6.85 ch., and *CB* = 6.10 ch.

9. Divide the five-sided field *ABCHE* among three persons, X, Y, and Z, in proportion to their claims, X paying $500, Y paying $750, and Z paying $1000, so that each may have the use of an interior pond at *P*, the quality of the land being equal throughout. Given *AB* = 8.64 ch., *BC* = 8.27 ch., *CH* = 8.06 ch., *HE* = 6.82 ch., and *EA* = 9.90 ch. The perpendicular *PD* upon *AB* = 5.60 ch., *PD'* upon *BC* = 6.08 ch., *PD''* upon *CH* = 4.80 ch., *PD'''* upon *HE* = 5.44 ch., and *PD''''* upon *EA* = 5.40 ch. Assume *PH* as the divisional fence between X's and Z's shares; it is required to determine the position of the fences *PM* and *PN* between X's and Y's shares and Y's and Z's shares, respectively.

10. Divide the triangular field *ABC*, whose sides *AB*, *AC*, and *BC* are 15, 12, and 10 ch., respectively, into three equal parts, by fences *EG* and *DF* parallel to *BC*, without finding the area of the field.

11. Divide the triangular field *ABC*, whose sides *AB*, *BC*, and *AC* are 22, 17, and 15 ch., respectively, among three persons, A, B, and C, by fences parallel to the base *AB*, so that A may have 3 A. above the line *AB*, B, 4 A. above A's share, and C, the remainder.

PLACE.	LATITUDE. Deg. Min.	LONGITUDE. Deg. Min.	VARIATION. 1800. Degrees.	1820. Degrees.	1840. Degrees.	1860. Degrees.	1880. Degrees.	1890. Degrees.	1895. Degrees.	ANNUAL CHANGE. 1895. Minutes.
Halifax N.S.	44 39.6	63 35.3	16.9	17.4	18.9	19.9	20.6	20.7	20.7	−0.2
Eastport, Me.	44 54.4	66 50.2	13.2	14.8	16.4	17.70	18.71	18.92	19.0	0.2
Bangor, Me.	44 48.2	68 46.9	10.9	12.1	13.7	15.3	16.54	16.99	17.2	1.7
Provincetown, Mass.	42 03.1	70 11.3	7.2	8.2	9.61	11.00	12.12	12.51	12.65	1.5
Portland, Me.	43 38.8	70 16.6	8.50	9.46	10.82	12.29	13.58	14.08	14.3	2.2
Portsmouth, N.H.	43 04.3	70 42.5	7.6	8.3	9.55	11.03	12.40	12.94	13.1	2.5
Boston, Mass.	42 21.5	71 03.9	6.90	7.78	9.01	10.33	11.47	11.9	12.1	1.9
Cambridge, Mass.	42 22.9	71 07.7	7.10	7.97	9.29	10.63	11.69	11.9	12.0	1.2
Quebec, Canada	46 48.4	71 14.5	12.1	12.3	13.8	16.0	17.4	17.5	17.5	−0.9
Providence, R.I.	41 50.2	71 23.8	6.40	6.71	8.24	9.78	10.70	11.56	11.9	3.6
Hartford, Conn.	41 46.9	72 40.4	5.10	5.58	6.69	7.93	9.29	9.89	10.2	3.0
New Haven, Conn.	41 18.5	72 55.7	4.7	5.0	5.95	7.35	8.84	9.52	9.8	3.4
Burlington, Vt.	44 28.5	73 12.0	7.2	7.78	8.90	10.27	11.58	12.11	12.3	2.4
Williamstown, Mass.	42 42.8	73 13.4	5.7	6.3	7.4	8.8	10.3	10.9	11.2	3.0
Montreal, Canada	45 30.5	73 34.6	8.0	7.9	9.4	12.0	13.8	14.4	14.7	3.4
Albany, N.Y.	42 39.2	73 45.8	5.5	6.02	7.07	8.44	9.87	10.52	10.82	3.4
New York, N.Y.	40 42.7	74 00.4	4.3	4.61	5.61	6.91	7.90	8.49	8.8	3.8
New Brunswick, N.J.	40 29.9	74 26.8	2.54	3.43	4.06	5.98	7.12	7.55	7.72	1.8
Cape Henlopen, Del.	38 46.7	75 05.0	0.8	1.1	2.00	3.36	4.86	5.6	5.9	3.7
Philadelphia, Pa.	39 56.9	75 09.0	2.1	2.44	3.46	4.73	6.20	6.97	7.4	4.4
Cape Henry, Va.	36 55.6	76 00.4	0.24	0.26	0.82	1.80	2.94	3.5	3.7	2.8
Ithaca, N.Y.	42 26.8	76 28.9	3.3	2.7	3.1	4.1	5.71	6.68	7.0	5.2
Baltimore, Md.	39 17.8	76 37.0	0.64	0.88	1.70	2.90	4.17	4.74	5.00	2.8
Williamsburg, Va.	37 16.2	76 42.4	−0.17	−0.22	0.38	1.47	2.75	3.3	3.6	3.2
Harrisburg, Pa.	40 16.9	76 52.9	0.0	0.8	2.2	3.71	5.05	5.52	5.7	1.8
Washington, D.C.	38 53.3	77 00.6	−0.1	0.3	1.19	2.42	3.66	4.18	4.40	3.0
Newbern, N.C.	35 06.0	77 02.0	−2.1	−1.06	−0.70	0.54	1.74	2.25	2.45	2.3
Buffalo, N.Y.	42 52.8	78 53.5	0.22	0.41	1.35	2.84	4.61	5.30	5.66	4.2
Toronto, Canada	43 39.4	79 23.5	....	....	1.32	2.17	3.62	4.12	4.5	4.4

Place	Latitude (Deg. Min.)	Longitude (Deg. Min.)	1800	1820	1840	1860	1880	1890	1895	Annual Change 1895 (Minutes)
Charleston, S.C.	32 46.0	79 55.8	-4.65	-4.05	-3.03	-1.73	-0.45	0.09	0.3	2.5
Pittsburg, Pa.	40 27.0	80 00.8	....	....	0.18	1.26	2.49	3.06	3.3	3.0
Erie, Pa.	42 07.8	80 05.4	-0.46	-0.39	0.36	1.60	2.99	3.02	3.9	3.2
Savannah, Ga.	32 04.9	81 06.5	....	-4.7	-4.2	-3.27	-2.06	-1.46	-1.2	3.4
Cleveland, O.	41 30.4	81 41.5	-1.8	-1.4	-0.60	0.39	1.62	2.06	2.29	2.8
Key West, Fla.	24 33.5	81 48.5	....	-0.86	-0.03	-0.85	-3.57	-2.90	-2.7	3.2
Detroit, Mich.	42 20.0	83 03.0	-3.1	-2.84	-2.04	-0.93	0.23	0.74	0.90	2.5
Sault Ste. Marie, Mich.	46 29.9	84 20.1	-0.5	-1.1	-1.04	0.34	0.84	1.52	1.9	4.1
Cincinnati, O.	39 08.4	84 25.3	-4.89	-4.99	-4.51	-3.57	-2.39	-1.80	-1.63	3.3
Grand Haven, Mich.	43 05.2	86 12.6	....	-6.0	-6.2	-4.46	-2.73	-1.6	-1.0	....
Nashville, Tenn.	36 08.9	86 48.2	....	-0.7	-0.9	-6.3	-5.13	-4.40	-4.0	4.7
Michigan City, Ind.	41 43.4	86 54.4	-0.84	....	-5.4	-5.13	-3.6	-2.0	-2.0	3.4
Pensacola, Fla.	30 20.8	87 18.3	....	-7.50	-7.13	-7.6	-6.34	-4.50	-4.20	4.6
Chicago, Ill.	41 50.0	87 30.8	....	-0.1	-0.2	-4.6	-4.62	-3.81	-3.45	4.4
Milwaukee, Wis.	43 02.5	87 54.2	-5.81	-6.71	-7.07	-6.05	-5.84	-5.23	-4.1	4.5
Mobile, Ala.	30 41.4	88 02.5	-7.12	-7.96	-8.16	-5.7	-5.84	-6.01	-4.9	4.0
New Orleans, La.	29 57.2	90 03.0	....	....	-8.6	-7.7	-6.50	-6.6	-5.6	4.3
St. Louis, Mo.	38 38.0	90 12.2	....	....	....	-7.7	-6.4	-6.0	-5.3	4.3
Duluth, Minn.	46 45.6	92 04.5	....	....	....	-10.02	-10.06	-9.0	-9.7	....
Galveston, Tex.	29 17.4	94 47.0	....	-12.6	-12.33	-8.84	-8.16	-7.50	-7.20	4.6
Omaha, Neb.	41 15.7	95 56.5	....	....	-10.7	-11.47	-10.23	-9.56	-9.21	4.1
Austin, Tex.	30 16.4	97 44.2	-10.69	-9.8	-10.29	-9.74	-8.80	-8.34	-8.1	....
San Antonio, Tex.	29 26.8	98 27.0	....	....	....	-10.16	-8.80	-8.80	-8.50	3.7
Denver, Col.	39 45.3	104 59.6	....	....	....	-16.14	-14.62	-14.06	-13.8	3.4
Salt Lake City, Utah	40 46.1	111 53.8	....	....	-12.67	-16.45	-16.68	-16.3	-16.0	3.2
San Diego, Cal.	32 42.1	117 14.3	....	-11.70	....	-13.21	-13.32	-13.22	-13.12	1.3
Seattle, Wash.	47 35.9	122 20.0	....	....	....	-21.8	-22.28	-22.26	-22.2	1.3
San Francisco, Cal.	37 47.5	122 27.3	-13.6	-14.54	-15.42	-16.10	-16.51	-16.58	-16.59	0.1
C. Mendocino, Cal.	40 26.3	124 24.3	-16.1	-16.0	-16.0	-17.4	-17.49	-17.69	-17.7	0.6

§ 25. UNITED STATES PUBLIC LANDS.

Burt's Solar Compass.

This instrument, which is exhibited on the following page, may be used for most of the purposes of a compass or transit. Its most important use, however, is to run north and south lines in laying out the public lands.

A full description of the solar compass, with its principles, adjustments, and uses, forms the subject of a considerable volume, which should be in the hands of the surveyor who uses this instrument. The limits of our space will allow only a brief reference to its principal features.

The main plate and standards resemble these parts of the compass.

a is the *latitude arc*.

b is the *declination arc*.

h is an arm, on each end of which is a *solar lens* having its focus on a silvered plate on the other end.

c is the *hour arc*.

n is the *needle-box*, which has an arc of about 36°.

To run a north and south line with the solar compass. Set off the declination of the sun on the declination arc. Set off the latitude of the place (which may be determined by this instrument) on the latitude arc. Set the instrument over the station, level, and turn the sights in a north and south direction, approximately, by the needle. Turn the solar lens toward the sun, and bring the sun's image between the equatorial lines on the silvered plate. Allowance being made for refraction, the sights will then indicate a true north and south line.

BURT'S SOLAR COMPASS.

Laying Out the Public Lands.

The public lands north of the Ohio River and west of the Mississippi are generally laid out in townships approximately six miles square.

A **Principal Meridian**, or true north and south line, is first run by means of Burt's Solar Compass, and then an east and west line, called a **Base Line.**

Parallels to the base line are run at intervals of six miles, and north and south lines at the same intervals. Thus the tract would be divided into townships exactly six miles square, if it were not for the convergence of the meridians on account of the curvature of the earth.

The north and south lines, or meridians, are called **Range Lines.** The east and west lines, or parallels, are called **Township Lines.**

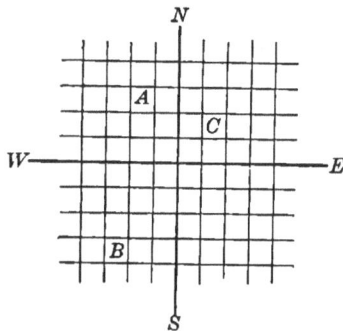

FIG. 33.

Let *NS* (Fig. 33) represent a principal meridian, and *WE* a base line; and let the other lines represent meridians and parallels at intervals of six miles.

The small squares, *A*, *B*, *C*, etc., will represent townships.

A would be designated thus: T. 3 N., R. 2 W.; that is, township three north, range two west; which means that the township is in the third tier north of the base line, and in the second tier west of the principal meridian. *B* and *C*, respectively, would be designated thus: T. 4 S., R. 3 W.; and T. 2 N., R. 2 E.

The townships are divided into sections approximately one mile square, and the sections are divided into quarter-sections. The township, section, and quarter-section corners are permanently marked.

6	5	4	3	2	1
7	8	9	10	11	12
18	17	16	15	14	13
19	20	21	22	23	24
30	29	28	27	26	25
31	32	33	34	35	36

FIG. 34.

The sections are numbered, beginning at the northeast corner, as in Fig. 34, which represents a township divided into sections. The quarter-sections are designated, according to their position, as N. E., N.W., S. E., and S.W.

Every fifth parallel is called a **Standard Parallel** or **Correction Line.**

Let NS (Fig. 35) represent a principal meridian ; WE a base line; rp, etc., meridians; and ms the fifth parallel. If Op equals six miles, mr will be less than six miles on account of the convergence of the meridians. Surveyors are instructed to make Op such a distance that mr shall be six miles; then mh, hk, etc., are taken similarly. At the correction lines north of ms the same operation is repeated.

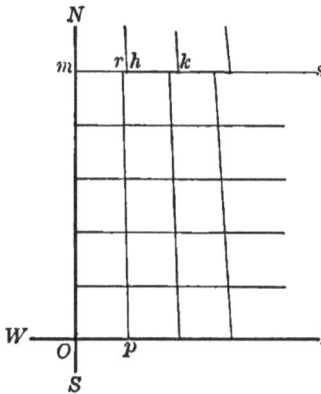

FIG. 35.

The township and section lines are surveyed in such an order as to throw the errors on the north and outer townships and sections.

If, in running a line, a navigable stream or a lake more than one mile in length is encountered, it is *meandered* by marking the intersection of the line with the bank and running lines from this point along the bank to prominent points which are marked, and the lengths and bearings of the connecting lines recorded.

Six principal meridians have been established and connected. In addition to these there are several independent meridians in the Western States and Territories which will in time be connected with each other and with the eastern system.

§ 26. PLANE-TABLE SURVEYING.*

After the principal lines of a survey have been determined and plotted, the details of the plot may be filled in by means of the plane-table ; or, when a plot only of a tract of land is desired, this instrument affords the most expeditious means of obtaining it.

An approved form of the plane-table, as used in the United States Coast and Geodetic Survey, is shown in the plate on page 243.

The **Table-top** is a board of well-seasoned wood, panelled with the grain at right angles to prevent warping, and supported at a convenient height by a **Tripod** and **Levelling Head**.

The **Alidade** is a ruler of brass or steel supporting a telescope or sight standards, whose line of sight is parallel to a plane perpendicular to the lower side of the ruler, and embracing its fiducial edge.

The **Declinatoire** consists of a detached rectangular box containing a magnetic needle which moves over an arc of about 10° on each side of the 0 point.

* In preparing this section the writer has consulted, by permission, the treatise on the plane-table by Mr. E. Hergesheimer, contained in the report for 1880 of the U.S. Coast and Geodetic Survey.

Two spirit levels at right angles are attached to the ruler or to the declinatoire. In some instruments these are replaced by a circular level, or by a detached spring level.

The paper upon which the plot is to be made or completed is fastened evenly to the board by clamps, the surplus paper being loosely rolled under the sides of the board.

To place the table in position. This operation, which is sometimes called orienting the table, consists in placing the table so that the lines of the plot shall be parallel to the corresponding lines on the ground.

This may be accomplished approximately by turning the table until the needle of the declinatoire indicates the same bearing as at a previous station, the edge of the declinatoire coinciding with the same line on the paper at both stations.

If, however, the line connecting the station at which the instrument is placed with another station is already plotted, the table may be placed in position accurately by placing it over the station so that the plotted line is by estimation over and in the direction of the line on the ground; then making the edge of the ruler coincide with the plotted line, and turning the board until the line of sight bisects the signal at the other end of the line on the ground.

To plot any point. Let ab on the paper represent the line AB on the ground; it is required to plot c, representing C on the ground.

1. *By intersection.*

Place the table in position at A (Fig. 36), plumbing a over A, and making the fiducial edge of the ruler pass through a; turn the alidade about a until the line of sight bisects the signal at C, and draw a line along the fiducial edge of the ruler. Place the table in position at B, plumbing b over B, and repeat the operation just described. c will be the intersection of the two lines thus drawn.

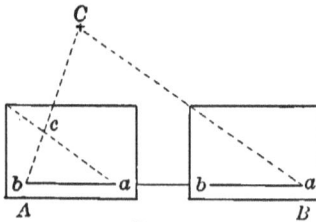

Fig. 36.

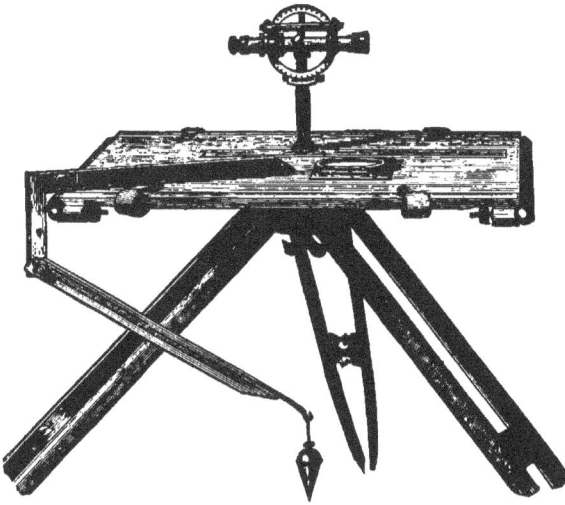

THE PLANE-TABLE.

2. By resection.

Place the table in position at A (Fig. 37), and draw a line in the direction of C, as in the former case; then remove the instrument to C, place it in position by the line drawn from a, make the edge of the ruler pass through b, and turn the alidade about b until B is in the line of sight. A line drawn along the edge of the ruler will intersect the line from a in c.

3. By radiation.

Place the table in position at A (Fig. 38), and draw a line from a toward C, as in the former cases. Measure AC, and lay off ac to the same scale as ab.

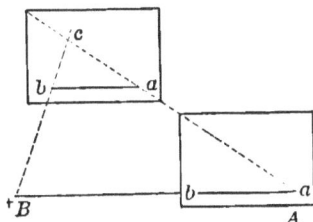

FIG. 37.

To plot a field $ABCD$.....

1. By radiation.

Set up the table at any point P, and mark p on the paper over P. Draw indefinite lines from p toward A, B, C ..... Measure PA, PB, ..., and lay off pa, pb, ..., to a suitable scale, and join a and b, b and c, c and d, etc.

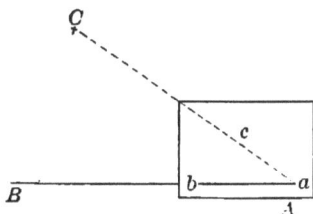

FIG. 38.

2. By progression.

Set up the table at A, and draw a line from a toward B. Measure AB, and plot ab to a suitable scale. Set up the table in position at B, and in like manner determine and plot bc, etc.

3. By intersection.

Plot one side as a base line. Plot the other corners by the method of intersection, and join.

4. By resection.

Plot one side as a base line. Plot the other corners by the method of resection, and join.

The Three Point Problem.

Let A, B, C represent three field stations plotted as a, b, c, respectively (Fig. 39); it is required to plot d representing a fourth field station D, visible from A, B, and C.

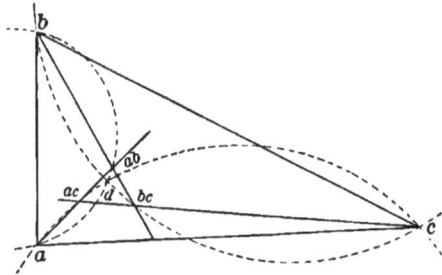

FIG. 39.

Place the table over D, level and orient approximately by the declinatoire. Determine d by resection as follows: Make the edge of the ruler pass through a and lie in the direction aA, and draw a line along the edge of the ruler. In like manner, draw lines through b toward B and through c toward C. If the table were oriented perfectly these lines would meet at the required point d, but ordinarily they will form the *triangle of error*, ab, ac, bc. In this case, through a, b, and ab; a, c, and ac; and b, c, and bc, respectively, draw circles; these circles will intersect in the required point d. For at the required point the sides ab, ac, bc must subtend the same angle as at the points ab, ac, bc, respectively. Hence, the required point d lies at the intersection of the three circles mentioned. The plane-table may now be oriented accurately.

NOTE. The three point problem may be solved by fastening on the board a piece of tracing paper and marking the point d representing D, after which lines are drawn from d toward A, B, and C. The tracing paper is then moved until the lines thus drawn pass through a, b, c, respectively, when by pricking through d the point is determined on the plot below.

CHAPTER III.

TRIANGULATION.*

§ 27. INTRODUCTORY REMARKS.

Geographical positions upon the surface of the earth are commonly determined by systems of triangles which connect a carefully determined base line with the points to be located.

Let F (Fig. 40) represent a point whose position with reference to the base line AB is required. Connect AB with F by the series of triangles ABC, ACD, ADE, and DEF, so that a signal at C is visible from A and B, a signal at D visible from A and C, a signal

FIG. 40.

at E visible from A and D, and a signal at F visible from D and E. In the triangle ABC, the side AB is known, and the angles at A and B may be measured; hence, AC may be computed. In the triangle ACD, AC is known, and the angles at A and C may be measured; hence, AD may be computed. In like manner DE and EF or DF may be determined. DF, or some suitable line connected with DF, may be measured, and this result compared with the computed value to test the accuracy of the field measurements.

* In preparing this chapter the writer has consulted, by permission, recent reports of the United States Coast and Geodetic Survey.

Three orders of triangulation are recognized, viz.:

Primary, in which the sides are from 20 to 150 miles in length.

Secondary, in which the sides are from 5 to 40 miles in length, and which connect the primary with the tertiary.

Tertiary, in which the sides are seldom over 5 miles in length, and which bring the survey down to such dimensions as to admit of the minor details being filled in by the compass and plane-table.

§ 28. The Measurement of Base Lines.

Base lines should be measured with a degree of accuracy corresponding to their importance.

Suitable ground must be selected and cleared of all obstructions.   Each extremity of the line may be marked by cross lines on the head of a copper tack driven into a stub which is sunk to the surface of the ground.   Poles are set up in line about half a mile apart, the alignment being controlled by a transit placed over one end of the line.

The *preliminary measurement* may be made with an iron wire about one-eighth of an inch in diameter and 60^m in length.   In measuring, the wire is brought into line by means of a transit set up in line not more than one-fourth of a mile in the rear.   The end of each 60^m is marked with pencil lines on a wooden bench whose legs are thrust into the ground after its position has been approximately determined.   If the last measurement exceeds or falls short of the extremity of the line, the difference may be measured with the 20^m chain.

The *final measurement* is made with the *base apparatus*, which consists of bars 6^m long, which are supported upon trestles when in use.   These bars are placed end to end, and brought to a horizontal position, if this can be quickly accomplished; if not, the angle of inclination is taken by a sector, or a vertical offset is measured with the aid of a transit, so that the exact horizontal distance can be computed.

A thermometer is attached to each bar, so that the temperature of the bar may be noted and a correction for temperature applied.

The method of measuring lines varies according to the required degree of accuracy in any particular case, but the brief description given above will give the student a general idea of the methods employed.

§ 29. THE MEASUREMENT OF ANGLES.

Angles are measured by the transit with much greater accuracy than by the compass, since the reading of the plates of the transit is taken to minutes, and by means of microscopes to seconds, while the reading of the needle of the compass is to quarter or half-quarter degrees.

In order to eliminate errors of observation, and errors arising from imperfect graduation of the circles, a large number of readings is made and their mean taken. Two methods are in use; viz., repetition and series.

The method of *repetition* consists, essentially, in measuring the angles about a point singly, then taking two adjacent angles as a single angle, then three, etc.; thus "closing the horizon," or measuring the whole angular magnitude about a point in several different ways.

The method of *series* consists, essentially, in taking the readings of an angle with the circle or limb of the transit in one position, then turning the circle through an arc and taking the readings of the same circle again, etc.; thus reading the angle from successive portions of the graduated circle.

On account of the curvature of the earth, the sum of the three angles of a triangle upon its surface exceeds 180°. This *spherical excess*, as it is called, becomes appreciable only when the sides of the triangle are about 5 miles in length. To determine the angles of the rectilinear triangle having the same vertices, one-third of the spherical excess is deducted from each spherical angle.

CHAPTER IV.

LEVELLING.

§ 30. DEFINITIONS, CURVATURE, AND REFRACTION.

A **Level Surface** is a surface parallel with the surface of still water; and is, therefore, slightly curved, owing to the spheroidal shape of the earth.

A **Level Line** is a line in a level surface.

Levelling is the process of finding the difference of level of two places, or the distance of one place above or below a level line through another place.

The **Line of Apparent Level** of a place is a tangent to the level line at that place. Hence, the line of apparent level is perpendicular to the plumb-line.

The **Correction for Curvature** is the deviation of the line of apparent level from the level line for any distance.

Let t (Fig. 41) represent the line of apparent level of the place P, a the level line, d the diameter of the earth; then c represents the correction for curvature. To compute the correction for curvature:

$$t^2 = c(c+d). \text{ (Geom. § 348.)}$$

Therefore, $c = \dfrac{t^2}{c+d} = \dfrac{a^2}{d}$

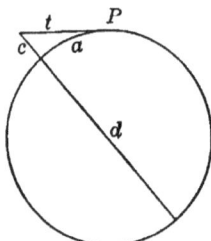

FIG. 41.

approximately, since c is very small compared with d, and $t = a$ without appreciable error.

Since d is constant ($= 7920$ miles, nearly), the correction for curvature varies as the square of the distance.

EXAMPLE. What is the correction for curvature for 1 mile ?
By substituting in the formula deduced above,

$$c = \frac{a^2}{d} = \frac{1^2}{7920} \text{ mi.} = 8 \text{ in.}$$

Hence, the correction for curvature for any distance may be found in inches, approximately, by multiplying 8 by the square of the distance expressed in miles.

NOTE. The effect of curvature is to make an object appear lower than it really is ; and the effect of refraction of light, caused by the greater density of the atmosphere near the surface of the earth, is to make an object appear higher than it really is. When both effects are taken into account c is more correctly expressed by $c = \frac{6}{7}$ of $\frac{a^2}{d}$.

§ 31. THE Y LEVEL.

This instrument is shown on page 253.

The *telescope* is about 20 inches in length, and rests on supports called Y's, from their shape. The *spirit level* is underneath the telescope, and attached to it. The *levelling-head* and *tripod* are similar to the same parts of the transit.

§ 32. THE LEVELLING ROD.

The two ends of the Philadelphia levelling rod are shown in Fig. 42. The rod is made of two pieces of wood, sliding upon each other, and held together in any position by a clamp.

The front surface of the rod is graduated to hundredths of a foot up to 7 feet. If a greater height than 7 feet is desired, the back part of the rod is moved up until the target is at the required height. When the rod is extended to full length, the front surface of the rear half reads from 7 to

FIG. 42.

13 feet, so that the rod becomes a self-reading rod 13 feet long.

The target slides along the front of the rod, and is held in place by two springs which press upon the sides of the rod. It has a square opening at the centre, through which the division line of the rod opposite to the horizontal line of the target may be seen. It carries a vernier by which heights may be read to thousandths of a foot (§ 7).

§ 33. DIFFERENCE OF LEVEL.

To find the difference of level between two places visible from an intermediate place, when the difference of level does not exceed 13 feet.

Let A and B (Fig. 43) represent the two places. Set the Y level at a station equally distant, or nearly so, from A and

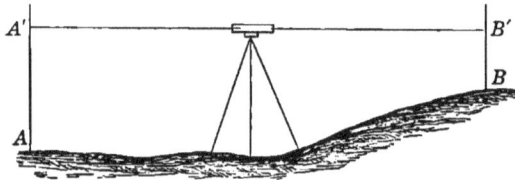

FIG. 43.

B, but not necessarily on the line AB. Place the legs of the tripod firmly in the ground, and level over each opposite pair of levelling screws, successively. Let the rodman hold the levelling rod vertically at A. Bring the telescope to bear upon the rod (§ 8), and by signal direct the rodman to move the target until its horizontal line is in the line of apparent level of the telescope. Let the rodman now record the height AA' of the target. In like manner find BB'. The difference between AA' and BB' will be the difference of level required. If the instrument is equally distant from A and B, or nearly so, the curvature and the refraction on the two sides of the instrument balance, and no correction for curvature or refraction will be necessary.

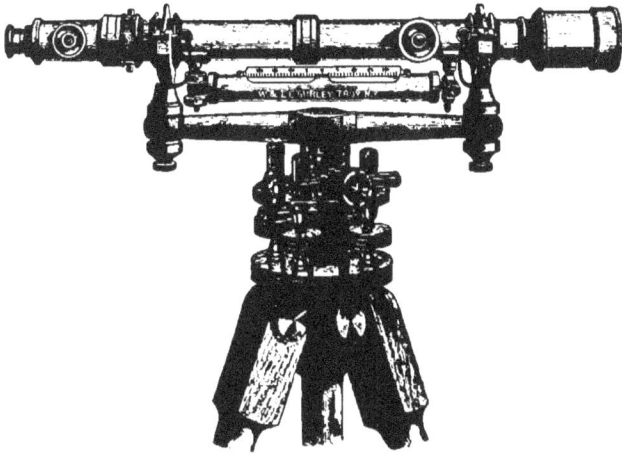

THE Y LEVEL.

If the instrument be set up at one station, and the rod at the other, the difference between the heights of the optical axis of the telescope and the target, corrected for curvature and refraction, will be the difference of level required.

To find the difference of level of two places, one of which cannot be seen from the other, and both invisible from the same place; or, when the two places differ considerably in level.

Let A and D (Fig. 44) represent the two places. Place the level midway between A and some intermediate station B.

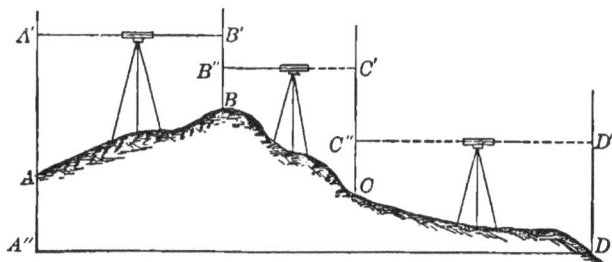

FIG. 44.

Find AA' and BB', as in the preceding case, and record the former as a *back-sight* and the latter as a *fore-sight*. Select another intermediate station C, and in like manner find the back-sight BB'' and the fore-sight CC'; and so continue until the place D is reached.

The difference between the sum of the fore-sights and the sum of the back-sights will be the difference of level required.

For, the sum of the fore-sights
$$= BB' + CC' + DD'$$
$$= BB'' + B'B'' + CC'' + C'C'' + DD'.$$
The sum of the back-sights
$$= AA' + BB'' + CC''.$$
Hence, the difference $= B'B'' + C'C'' + DD' - AA'$
$$= A'A'' - AA' = AA''.$$

§ 34. LEVELLING FOR SECTION.

The intersection of a vertical plane with the surface of the earth is called a **Section** or **Profile.** The term profile, however, usually designates the **Plot** or representation of the section on paper.

Levelling for Section is levelling to obtain the data necessary for making a profile or plot of any required section.

A profile is made for the purpose of exhibiting in a single view the inequalities of the surface of the ground for great distances along the line of some proposed improvement, such as a railroad, canal, or ditch, and thus facilitating the establishment of the proper grades.

The data necessary for making a profile of any required section are, the heights of its different points above some assumed horizontal plane, called the **Datum Plane,** together with their horizontal distances apart or from the beginning of the section.

The position of the datum plane is fixed with reference to some permanent object near the beginning of the section, called a **Bench Mark,** and, in order to avoid negative heights, is assumed at such a distance below this mark that all the points of the section shall be above it.

The heights of the different points of the section above the datum plane are determined by means of the level and levelling-rod; and the horizontal length of the section is measured with an engineer's chain or tape, and divided into equal parts, one hundred feet in length, called **Stations,** marked by stakes numbered 0, 1, 2, 3, etc.

Where the ground is very irregular, it may be necessary, besides taking sights at the regular stakes, to take occasional sights at points between them. If, for instance, at a point sixty feet in advance of stake 8 there is a sudden rise or fall in the surface, the height of this point would be determined and recorded as at stake 8.60.

The readings of the rod are ordinarily taken to the nearest tenth of a foot, except on *bench marks* and points called *turning points*, where they are taken to thousandths of a foot.

A **Turning Point** is a point on which the last sight is taken just before changing the position of the level, and the first sight from the new position of the instrument. A turning point may be coincident with one of the stakes, but must always be a hard point, so that the foot of the rod may stand at the same level for both readings.

To explain the method of obtaining the field notes necessary for making a profile, let 0, 1, 2, 3, ... 11 (Fig. 45) represent a portion of a section to be levelled and plotted. Establish a bench mark at or near the beginning of the line, measure the horizontal length of the section, and set stakes one hundred feet apart, numbering them 0, 1, 2, 3, etc. Place the level at some point, as between 2 and 3, and take the reading of the rod on the bench = 4.832. Let PP' represent the datum plane, say 15 feet below the bench mark, then

$$15 + 4.832 = 19.832$$

will be the height of the line of sight AB, called the **Height of the Instrument,** above the datum plane. Now take the reading at $0 = 5.2 = 0A$, and subtract the same from 19.832, which

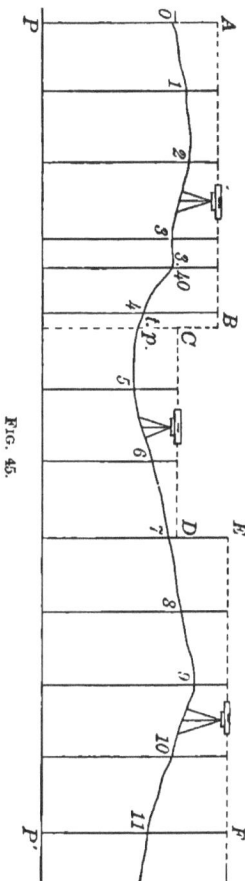

leaves $14.6 = 0P$, the height of the point 0 above the datum plane. Next take sights at 1, 2, 3, 3.40, and 4 equal respectively to 3.7, 3.0, 5.1, 4.8, and 8.3, and subtract the same from 19.832; the remainders 16.1, 16.8, 14.7, 15.0, and 11.5 will be the respective heights of the points 1, 2, 3, 3.40, and 4. Then, as it will be necessary to change the position of the instrument, select a point in the neighborhood of 4 suitable as a turning point (*t.p.* in the figure), and take a careful reading on it $= 8.480$; subtract this from 19.832, and the remainder, 11.352, will be the height of the turning point. Now carry the instrument forward to a new position, as between 5 and 6, shown in the figure, while the rodman remains at *t.p.*; take a second reading on $t.p. = 4.102$, and add it to 11.352, the height of *t.p.* above PP'; the sum 15.454 will be the height of the instrument CD in its new position. Now take sight upon 5, 6, and 7, equal respectively to 4.9, 2.8, and 0.904; subtract these sights from 15.454, and the results 10.6, 12.7, and 14.550 will be the heights of the points 5, 6, and 7 respectively. The point 7, being suitable, is made a turning point, and the instrument is moved forward to a point between 9 and 10. The sight at $7 = 6.870$ added to the height of 7 gives 21.420 as the height of the instrument EF in its new position. The readings at 8, 9, 10, and 11, which are respectively 5.4, 3.6, 5.8, and 9.0, subtracted from 21.420, will give the heights of these points, namely, 16.0, 17.8, 15.6, and 12.4.

Proceed in like manner until the entire section is levelled, establishing bench marks at intervals along the line to serve as reference points for future operations.

As wind and bright sunshine affect the accuracy of levelling, for careful work a calm and cloudy day should be chosen; and great pains be taken to hold the rod vertical and to manipulate the level properly.

A record of the work described above is kept as follows:

STATION.	+ S.	H.I.	− S.	H.S.	REMARKS.
B	4.832			15.	Bench on rock 20 ft.
0		19.832	5.2	14.6	south of 0.
1			3.7	16.1	
2			3.0	16.8	
3			5.1	14.7	3 to 3.40 turnpike road.
3.40			4.8	15.0	
4			8.3	11.5	
t.p.	4.102		8.480	11.352	
5		15.454	4.9	10.6	
6			2.8	12.7	
7	6.870		0.904	14.550	
8		21.420	5.4	16.0	
9			3.6	17.8	
10			5.8	15.6	
11			9.0	12.4	
B					Bench on oak stump
12					27 ft. N.E. of 12,
etc.					etc.

The first column contains the numbers or names of all the points on which sights are taken. The second column contains the sight taken on the first bench mark, and the sight on each turning point taken immediately after the instrument has been moved to a new position. These are called **Plus Sights** ($+ S.$) because they are **added** to the heights of the points on which they are taken to obtain the height of the instrument given in the third column ($H.I.$). The fourth column contains all the readings except those recorded in the second column. These are called **Minus Sights** ($- S.$) because they are **subtracted** from the numbers in the third column to obtain all the numbers in the fifth column except the first, which is the assumed depth of the datum plane below the bench. The fifth column ($H.S.$, height of surface) contains the required heights of all the points of the section named in the first column together with the heights of all benches and turning points.

To find the difference of level between any two points of the section, we have only to take the difference between the numbers in the fifth column opposite these points.

The real field notes are contained in the first, second, fourth, and last columns; the other columns may be filled after the field operations are completed. The field book may contain other columns; one for **height of grade** (*H.G.*), another for **depth of cut** (*C.*) and another for **height of embankment** or **fill** (*F.*).

To plot the section. Draw a line *PP'* (Fig. 45), to represent the datum plane, and beginning at some point as *P*, lay off the distances 100, 200, 300, 340, 400 feet, etc., to the right, using some convenient scale, say 200 feet to the inch. At these points of division erect perpendiculars equal in length to the height of the points 0, 1, 2, 3.40, 4, etc., given in the fifth column of the above field notes, using in this case a larger scale, say 20 feet to the inch. Through the extremities of these perpendiculars draw the irregular line 0, 1, 2, 3 ..... 11, and the result, with some explanatory figures, will be the required plot or profile.

The making of a profile is much simplified by the use of *profile paper*, which may be had by the yard or roll.

If a *horizontal plot* is required, the bearings of the different portions of the section must be taken.

A plot should be made, if it will assist in properly understanding the field work, or if it is desirable for future reference in connection with the field notes.

§ 35. SUBSTITUTES FOR THE Y LEVEL.

For many purposes not requiring accuracy, the following simple instruments in connection with a graduated rod will be found sufficient.

The **Plumb Level** (Fig. 46) consists of two pieces of wood joined at right angles. A straight line is drawn on the upright perpendicular to the upper edge of the cross-head.

The instrument is fastened to a support by a screw through the centre of the cross-head. The upper edge of the cross-head is brought to a level by making the line on the upright coincide with a plumb-line.

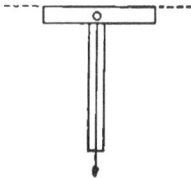 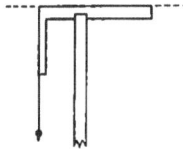 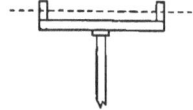

FIG. 46.   FIG. 47.   FIG. 48.

A modified form is shown in Fig. 47. A carpenter's square is supported by a post, the top of which is split or sawed so as to receive the longer arm. The shorter arm is made vertical by a plumb-line which brings the longer arm to a level.

The **Water Level** is shown in Fig. 48. The upright tubes are of glass, cemented into a connecting tube of any suitable material. The whole is nearly filled with water, and supported at a convenient height. The surface of the water in the uprights determines the level.

By sighting along the upper surface of the block in which the **Spirit Level** is mounted for the use of mechanics, a level line may be obtained.

EXERCISE V.

1. Find the difference of level of two places from the following field notes : back-sights, 5.2, 6.8, and 4.0 ; fore-sights, 8.1, 9.5, and 7.9.

2. Write the proper numbers in the third and fifth columns of the following table of field notes, and make a profile of the section :

STATION.	+ S.	H.I.	− S.	H.S.	REMARKS.
B	6.944			20	Bench on post 22 ft.
0			7.4		north of 0.
1			5.6		
2			3.9		
3			4.6		
t.p.	3.855		5.513		'
4			4.9		
5			3.5		
6			1.2		

3. Stake 0 of the following notes stands at the lowest point
of a pond to be drained into a creek; stake 10 stands at the
edge of the bank, and 10.25 at the bottom of the creek. Make
a profile, draw the grade line through 0 and 10.25, and fill
out the columns *H.G.* and *C.*, the former to show the height
of grade line above the datum, and the latter, the depth of
cut at the several stakes necessary to construct the drain.

STATION.	+ S.	H.I.	− S.	H.S.	H.G.	C.	REMARKS.
B	6.000			25			Bench on rock
0			10.2		20.8	0.0	30 feet west of
1			5.3			5.3	stake 1.
2			4.6				
3			4.0				
4			6.8				
5	4.572		7.000				
6			3.9				
7			2.0				
8			4.9				
9			4.3				
10			4.5				
10.25			11.8				

Horizontal scale, 2 ch. = 1 in.
Vertical scale,   20 ft. = 1 in.

§ 36. Topographical Levelling.

The principal object of topographical surveying is to show the contour of the ground. This operation, called topographical levelling, is performed by representing on paper the curved lines in which parallel horizontal planes at uniform distances apart would meet the surface.

It is evident that all points in the intersection of a horizontal plane with the surface of the ground are at the same level. Hence, it is only necessary to find points at the same level, and join these to determine a line of intersection.

The method commonly employed will be understood by a reference to Fig. 49. The ground $ABCD$ is divided into equal squares, and a numbered stake driven at each intersection. By means of a level and levelling rod the heights of the other stations above m and D, the lowest stations, are determined. A plot of the ground with the intersecting lines is then drawn, and the height of each station written as in the figure.

Suppose that the horizontal planes are 2 feet apart; if the first passes through m and D, the second will pass through p, which is 2 feet above m; and since n is 3 feet above m, the second plane will cut the line mn in a point s determined by the proportion $mn : ms :: 3 : 2$. In like manner the points t, q, and r are determined.

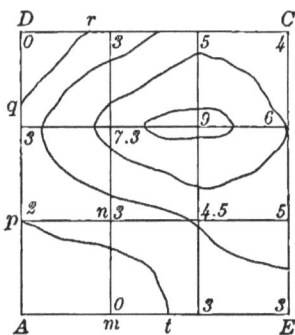

FIG. 49.

The irregular line tsp ..... qr represents the intersection of the second horizontal plane with the surface of the ground. In like manner the intersections of the planes, respectively, 4, 6, and 8 feet above m are traced. The more rapid the change in level the nearer these lines will approach each other.

CHAPTER V.

RAILROAD SURVEYING.

§ 37. General Remarks.

When the general route of a railroad has been determined, a middle surface line is run with the transit. A profile of this line is determined, as in § 34. The levelling stations are commonly 1 chain (100 feet) apart. Places of different level are connected by a gradient line, which intersects the perpendiculars to the datum line at the levelling stations in points determined by simple proportion. Hence, the distance of each levelling station, above or below the level or gradient line which represents the position of the road bed, is known.

§ 38. Cross Section Work.

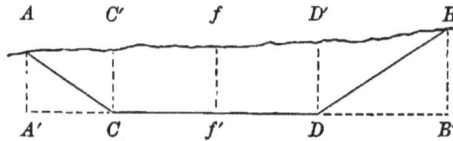

Fig. 50.

Excavations. If the road bed lies below the surface, an excavation is made.

Let $ACDB$ (Fig. 50) represent a cross section of an excavation, f a point in the middle surface line, f' the corresponding point in the road bed, and CD the width of the excavation at the bottom. The slopes at the sides are commonly made so that $AA' = \frac{2}{3} A'C$, and $BB' = \frac{2}{3} DB'$. ff' and CD being known, the points A, B, C', and D' are readily determined by a level and tape measure.

If from the area of the trapezoid $ABB'A'$ the areas of the triangles $AA'C$ and $BB'D$ be deducted, the remainder will be the area of the cross section.

In like manner the cross section at the next station may be determined. These two cross sections will be the bases of a frustum of a quadrangular pyramid whose volume will be the amount of the excavation, approximately.

Embankments. If the road bed lies above the surface, an embankment is made, the cross section of which is like that of the excavation, but inverted.

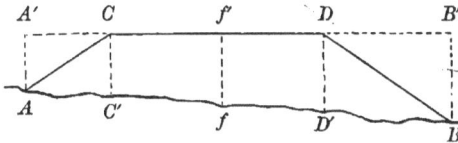

FIG. 51.

Fig. 51 represents the cross section of an embankment which is lettered so as to show its relation to Fig. 50.

§ 39. RAILROAD CURVES.

When it is necessary to change the direction of a railroad, it is done gradually by a curve, usually the arc of a circle.

Let AF and AO (Fig. 52) represent two lines to be thus connected. Take any convenient distance $AB = AE = t$. The intersection of the perpendiculars BC and EC deter-

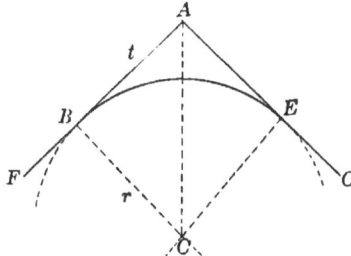

FIG. 52.

mines the centre C, and the radius of curvature $BC = r$. The length of the radius of curvature will depend on the angle A and the tangent AB. For, in the right triangle ABC,

$$\tan BAC = \frac{BC}{AB}, \quad \text{or } \tan \tfrac{1}{2}A = \frac{r}{t}.$$

Hence, $r = t \tan \tfrac{1}{2}A$.

The *degree* of a railroad curve is the angle subtended at the centre of the curve by a chord of 100 feet. If D is the degree of a curve and r its radius,

$$\sin \tfrac{1}{2}D = \frac{50}{r} \quad \text{and} \quad r = 50 \csc \tfrac{1}{2}D.$$

For example, a 6° curve has a radius of 955.37 feet.

To Lay out the Curve.

First Method. Let Bm (Fig. 53) represent a portion of the tangent. It is required to find mP, the perpendicular to the tangent meeting the curve at P.

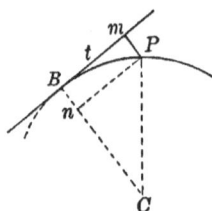

FIG. 53.

$$mP = Bn = CB - Cn.$$

But $\qquad CD = r,$

and $\qquad Cn = \sqrt{\overline{CP^2} - \overline{Pn^2}}$

$$= \sqrt{r^2 - t^2}.$$

Hence, $\qquad mP = r - \sqrt{r^2 - t^2}.$

Second Method. It is required to find mP (Fig. 54) in the direction of the centre.

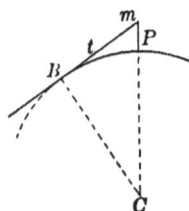

FIG. 54.

$$mP = mC - PC.$$

But $\quad mC = \sqrt{\overline{BC^2} + \overline{Bm^2}} = \sqrt{r^2 + t^2}.$

Hence,

$$mP = \sqrt{r^2 + t^2} - r.$$

Third Method. Place transits at B and E (Fig. 55). Direct the telescope of the former to E, and of the latter to A. Turn each toward the curve the same number of degrees, and mark P, the point of intersection of the lines of sight. P will be a point in the circle to which AB and AE are tangents at B and E, respectively.

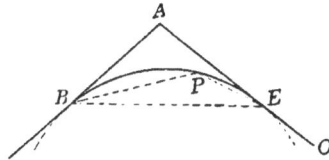

FIG. 55.

Fourth Method. If the degree D of the curve is given and the tangent BA at B (Fig. 56), place the transit at B and direct toward A. Turn off successively the angles $ABP, PBP', P'BP'', \ldots$ each equal to $\frac{1}{2}D$, and take DP, $PP', P'P'', \ldots$ each 100 ft., the length of the tape. Then $P, P', P'', \ldots$ lie on the required curve.

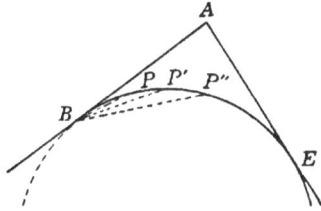

FIG. 56.

If the angle A and the tangent distance $BA = t$ are given, D can be found from the formulas

$$\sin \tfrac{1}{2}D = \frac{50}{r}, \quad r = t \tan \tfrac{1}{2}A, \quad \therefore \sin \tfrac{1}{2}D = \frac{50}{t} \cot \tfrac{1}{2}A.$$

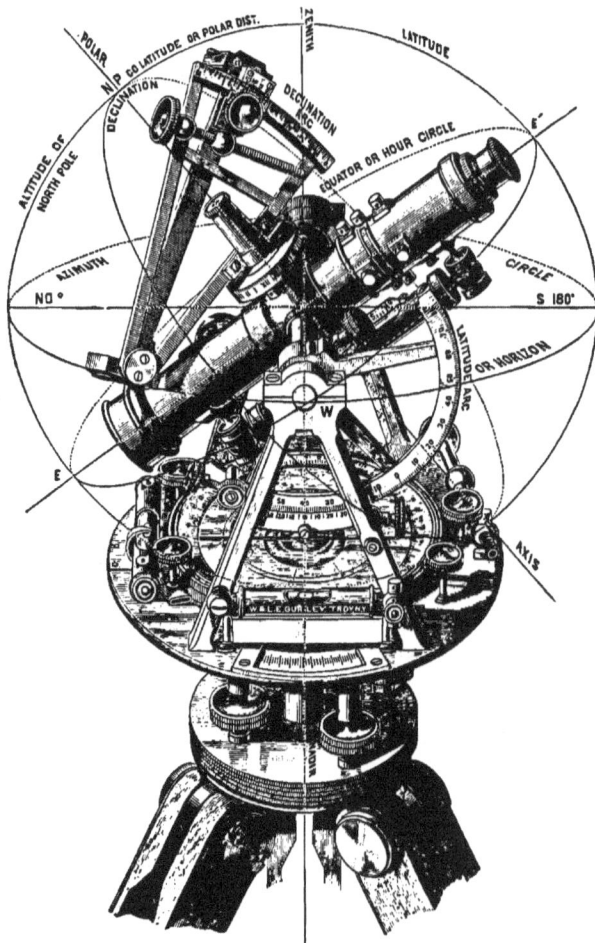

TRANSIT WITH SOLAR ATTACHMENT.

The circles shown in the cut are intended to represent in miniature circles supposed to be drawn upon the concave surface of the heavens.

SURVEYING.

Exercise I.

1. 8 A. 64 P.
2. 29 A. 7¾ P.
3. 4 A. 5$\frac{9}{25}$ P.
4. 115$\frac{7}{20}$ P.

5. 3 A. 78 P.
6. 13 A. 6$\frac{1}{10}$ P.
7. 11 A. 157 P.
8. 7.51925.

9. 13.0735.
10. 2 A. 58½ P.
11. 4 A. 35 P.

Exercise II.

1. 2 A. 26 P.
2. 20 A. 12 P.
3. 2 A. 54 P.
4. 2 A. 151 P.

5. 8 A. 54 P.
6. 5 A. 42 P.
7. 2 A. 78 P.

8. 3 A. 122 P.
9. 6 A. 2 P.
10. 9 A. 40 P.

Exercise III.

1. 2 A. 12½ P.

2. 98 A. 92 P.

Exercise IV.

1. $AE = 3.75$ ch.
2. $AE = 3.50$ ch. ;
   $EG = 3.42$ ch.
3. $AE = 4.55$ ch.
4. $AE = 5.50$ ch.
5. $CE = 4.456$ ch.
6. $AD = 2.275$ ch. ;
   $BE = 1.82$ ch.
7. $AD = 4.51$ ch. ;
   $BE = 3.61$ ch.
8. The distances on AB are 2, 3, and 5 ch.

9. EM (on EA) $= 2.5087$ ch. ;
   AN (on AB) $= 6.439$ ch.
10. Let $EG > DF$,
    then $\begin{cases} AE = 12.247 \text{ ch.} \\ AG = 9.798 \text{ ch.} \\ AD = 8.659 \text{ ch.} \\ AF = 6.928 \text{ ch.} \end{cases}$
11. Let $DG > EF$,
    then $\begin{cases} CG = 14.862 \text{ ch.} \\ CD = 13.113 \text{ ch.} \\ CF = 11.404 \text{ ch.} \\ CE = 10.062 \text{ ch.} \end{cases}$

EXERCISE V.

1. 9.5 feet.

2. Third column : 26.944 opposite 0 ; 25.286 opposite 4.
   Fifth column : 20, 19.5, 21.3, 23, 22.3, 21.431, 20.4, 21.8, 24.1.

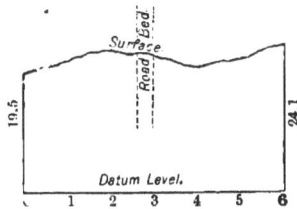

3. Column *H.G.* 20.8, 20.4, 20.0, 19.6, etc.
   Column *C.* 0.0, 5.3, 6.4, 7.4, 5.0, 5.1, etc.

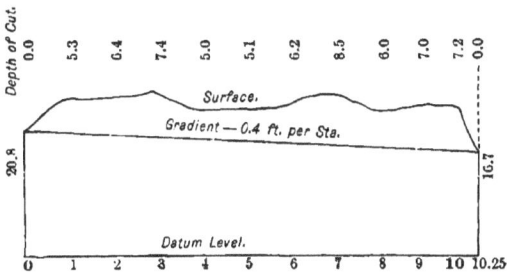

TABLE VII.—TRAVERSE TABLE.

Bearing.	Distance 1.		Distance 2.		Distance 3.		Distance 4.		Distance 5.		Bearing.
° ′	Lat.	Dep.	Lat.	Dep.	Lat.	Dep.	Lat.	Dep.	Lat.	Dep.	° ′
0 15	1.000	0.004	2.000	0.009	3.000	0.013	4.000	0.017	5.000	0.022	89 45
30	1.000	0.009	2.000	0.017	3.000	0.026	4.000	0.035	5.000	0.044	30
45	1.000	0.013	2.000	0.026	3.000	0.039	4.000	0.052	5.000	0.065	15
1 0	1.000	0.017	2.000	0.035	3.000	0.052	3.999	0.070	4.999	0.087	89 0
15	1.000	0.022	2.000	0.044	2.999	0.065	3.999	0.087	4.999	0.109	45
30	1.000	0.026	1.999	0.052	2.999	0.079	3.999	0.105	4.998	0.131	30
45	1.000	0.031	1.999	0.061	2.999	0.092	3.998	0.122	4.998	0.153	15
2 0	0.999	0.035	1.999	0.070	2.998	0.105	3.998	0.140	4.997	0.174	88 0
15	0.999	0.039	1.998	0.079	2.998	0.118	3.997	0.157	4.996	0.196	45
30	0.999	0.044	1.998	0.087	2.997	0.131	3.996	0.174	4.995	0.218	30
45	0.999	0.048	1.998	0.096	2.997	0.144	3.995	0.192	4.994	0.240	15
3 0	0.999	0.052	1.997	0.105	2.996	0.157	3.995	0.209	4.993	0.262	87 0
15	0.998	0.057	1.997	0.113	2.995	0.170	3.994	0.227	4.992	0.283	45
30	0.998	0.061	1.996	0.122	2.994	0.183	3.993	0.244	4.991	0.305	30
45	0.998	0.065	1.996	0.131	2.994	0.196	3.991	0.262	4.989	0.327	15
4 0	0.998	0.070	1.995	0.140	2.993	0.209	3.990	0.279	4.988	0.349	86 0
15	0.997	0.074	1.995	0.148	2.992	0.222	3.989	0.296	4.986	0.371	45
30	0.997	0.078	1.994	0.157	2.991	0.235	3.988	0.314	4.985	0.392	30
45	0.997	0.083	1.993	0.166	2.990	0.248	3.986	0.331	4.983	0.414	15
5 0	0.996	0.087	1.992	0.174	2.989	0.261	3.985	0.349	4.981	0.436	85 0
15	0.996	0.092	1.992	0.183	2.987	0.275	3.983	0.366	4.979	0.458	45
30	0.995	0.096	1.991	0.192	2.986	0.288	3.982	0.383	4.977	0.479	30
45	0.995	0.100	1.990	0.200	2.985	0.301	3.980	0.401	4.975	0.501	15
6 0	0.995	0.105	1.989	0.209	2.984	0.314	3.978	0.418	4.973	0.523	84 0
15	0.994	0.109	1.988	0.218	2.982	0.327	3.976	0.435	4.970	0.544	45
30	0.994	0.113	1.987	0.226	2.981	0.340	3.974	0.453	4.968	0.566	30
45	0.993	0.118	1.986	0.235	2.979	0.353	3.972	0.470	4.965	0.588	15
7 0	0.993	0.122	1.985	0.244	2.978	0.366	3.970	0.487	4.963	0.609	83 0
15	0.992	0.126	1.984	0.252	2.976	0.379	3.968	0.505	4.960	0.631	45
30	0.991	0.131	1.983	0.261	2.974	0.392	3.966	0.522	4.957	0.653	30
45	0.991	0.135	1.982	0.270	2.973	0.405	3.963	0.539	4.954	0.674	15
8 0	0.990	0.139	1.981	0.278	2.971	0.418	3.961	0.557	4.951	0.696	82 0
15	0.990	0.143	1.979	0.287	2.969	0.430	3.959	0.574	4.948	0.717	45
30	0.989	0.148	1.978	0.296	2.967	0.443	3.956	0.591	4.945	0.739	30
45	0.988	0.152	1.977	0.304	2.965	0.456	3.953	0.608	4.942	0.761	15
9 0	0.988	0.156	1.975	0.313	2.963	0.469	3.951	0.626	4.938	0.782	81 0
15	0.987	0.161	1.974	0.321	2.961	0.482	3.948	0.643	4.935	0.804	45
30	0.986	0.165	1.973	0.330	2.959	0.495	3.945	0.660	4.931	0.825	30
45	0.986	0.169	1.971	0.339	2.957	0.508	3.942	0.677	4.928	0.847	15
10 0	0.985	0.174	1.970	0.347	2.954	0.521	3.939	0.695	4.924	0.868	80 0
15	0.984	0.178	1.968	0.356	2.952	0.534	3.936	0.712	4.920	0.890	45
30	0.983	0.182	1.967	0.364	2.950	0.547	3.933	0.729	4.916	0.911	30
45	0.982	0.187	1.965	0.373	2.947	0.560	3.930	0.746	4.912	0.933	15
11 0	0.982	0.191	1.963	0.382	2.945	0.572	3.927	0.763	4.908	0.954	79 0
15	0.981	0.195	1.962	0.390	2.942	0.585	3.923	0.780	4.904	0.975	45
30	0.980	0.199	1.960	0.399	2.940	0.598	3.920	0.797	4.900	0.997	30
45	0.979	0.204	1.958	0.407	2.937	0.611	3.916	0.815	4.895	1.018	15
12 0	0.978	0.208	1.956	0.416	2.934	0.624	3.913	0.832	4.891	1.040	78 0
15	0.977	0.212	1.954	0.424	2.932	0.637	3.909	0.849	4.886	1.061	45
30	0.976	0.216	1.953	0.433	2.929	0.649	3.905	0.866	4.881	1.082	30
45	0.975	0.221	1.951	0.441	2.926	0.662	3.901	0.883	4.877	1.103	15
13 0	0.974	0.225	1.949	0.450	2.923	0.675	3.897	0.900	4.872	1.125	77 0
15	0.973	0.229	1.947	0.458	2.920	0.688	3.894	0.917	4.867	1.146	45
30	0.972	0.233	1.945	0.467	2.917	0.700	3.889	0.934	4.862	1.167	30
45	0.971	0.238	1.943	0.475	2.914	0.713	3.885	0.951	4.857	1.188	15
14 0	0.970	0.242	1.941	0.484	2.911	0.726	3.881	0.968	4.851	1.210	76 0
15	0.969	0.246	1.938	0.492	2.908	0.738	3.877	0.985	4.846	1.231	45
30	0.968	0.250	1.936	0.501	2.904	0.751	3.873	1.002	4.841	1.252	30
45	0.967	0.255	1.934	0.509	2.901	0.764	3.868	1.018	4.835	1.273	15
15 0	0.966	0.259	1.932	0.518	2.898	0.776	3.864	1.035	4.830	1.294	75 0
° ′	Dep.	Lat.	Dep.	Lat.	Dep.	Lat.	Dep.	Lat.	Dep.	Lat.	° ′
Bearing.	Distance 1.		Distance 2.		Distance 3.		Distance 4.		Distance 5.		Bearing.

Bearing.	Distance 6.		Distance 7.		Distance 8.		Distance 9.		Distance 10.		Bearing.
° ′	Lat.	Dep.	Lat.	Dep.	Lat.	Dep.	Lat.	Dep.	Lat.	Dep.	° ′
0 15	6.000	0.026	7.000	0.031	8.000	0.035	9.000	0.039	10.000	0.044	89 45
30	6.000	0.052	7.000	0.061	8.000	0.070	9.000	0.079	10.000	0.087	30
45	5.999	0.079	6.999	0.092	7.999	0.105	8.999	0.118	9.999	0.131	15
1 0	5.999	0.105	6.999	0.122	7.999	0.140	8.999	0.157	9.999	0.175	89 0
15	5.999	0.131	6.998	0.153	7.998	0.175	8.998	0.196	9.998	0.218	45
30	5.998	0.157	6.998	0.183	7.997	0.209	8.997	0.236	9.997	0.262	30
45	5.997	0.183	6.997	0.214	7.996	0.244	8.996	0.275	9.995	0.305	15
2 0	5.996	0.209	6.996	0.244	7.995	0.279	8.995	0.314	9.994	0.349	88 0
15	5.995	0.236	6.995	0.275	7.994	0.314	8.993	0.353	9.992	0.393	45
30	5.994	0.262	6.993	0.305	7.992	0.349	8.991	0.393	9.991	0.436	30
45	5.993	0.288	6.992	0.336	7.991	0.384	8.990	0.432	9.989	0.480	15
3 0	5.992	0.314	6.990	0.366	7.989	0.419	8.988	0.471	9.986	0.523	87 0
15	5.990	0.340	6.989	0.397	7.987	0.454	8.986	0.510	9.984	0.567	45
30	5.989	0.366	6.987	0.427	7.985	0.488	8.983	0.549	9.981	0.611	30
45	5.987	0.392	6.985	0.458	7.983	0.523	8.981	0.589	9.979	0.654	15
4 0	5.985	0.419	6.983	0.488	7.981	0.558	8.978	0.628	9.976	0.698	86 0
15	5.984	0.445	6.981	0.519	7.978	0.593	8.975	0.667	9.973	0.741	45
30	5.982	0.471	6.978	0.549	7.975	0.628	8.972	0.706	9.969	0.785	30
45	5.979	0.497	6.976	0.580	7.973	0.662	8.969	0.745	9.966	0.828	15
5 0	5.977	0.523	6.973	0.610	7.970	0.697	8.966	0.784	9.962	0.872	85 0
15	5.975	0.549	6.971	0.641	7.966	0.732	8.962	0.824	9.958	0.915	45
30	5.972	0.575	6.968	0.671	7.963	0.767	8.959	0.863	9.954	0.959	30
45	5.970	0.601	6.965	0.701	7.960	0.802	8.955	0.902	9.950	1.002	15
6 0	5.967	0.627	6.962	0.732	7.956	0.836	8.951	0.941	9.945	1.045	84 0
15	5.964	0.653	6.958	0.762	7.952	0.871	8.947	0.980	9.941	1.089	45
30	5.961	0.679	6.955	0.792	7.949	0.906	8.942	1.019	9.936	1.132	30
45	5.958	0.705	6.951	0.823	7.945	0.940	8.938	1.058	9.931	1.175	15
7 0	5.955	0.731	6.948	0.853	7.940	0.975	8.933	1.097	9.926	1.219	83 0
15	5.952	0.757	6.944	0.883	7.936	1.010	8.928	1.136	9.920	1.262	45
30	5.949	0.783	6.940	0.914	7.932	1.044	8.923	1.175	9.914	1.305	30
45	5.945	0.809	6.936	0.944	7.927	1.079	8.918	1.214	9.909	1.349	15
8 0	5.942	0.835	6.932	0.974	7.922	1.113	8.912	1.253	9.903	1.392	82 0
15	5.938	0.861	6.928	1.004	7.917	1.148	8.907	1.291	9.897	1.435	45
30	5.934	0.887	6.923	1.035	7.912	1.182	8.901	1.330	9.890	1.478	30
45	5.930	0.913	6.919	1.065	7.907	1.217	8.895	1.369	9.884	1.521	15
9 0	5.926	0.939	6.914	1.095	7.902	1.251	8.889	1.408	9.877	1.564	81 0
15	5.922	0.964	6.909	1.125	7.896	1.286	8.883	1.447	9.870	1.607	45
30	5.918	0.990	6.904	1.155	7.890	1.320	8.877	1.485	9.863	1.651	30
45	5.913	1.016	6.899	1.185	7.884	1.355	8.870	1.524	9.856	1.694	15
10 0	5.909	1.042	6.894	1.216	7.878	1.389	8.863	1.563	9.848	1.737	80 0
15	5.904	1.068	6.888	1.246	7.872	1.424	8.856	1.601	9.840	1.779	45
30	5.900	1.093	6.883	1.276	7.866	1.458	8.849	1.640	9.833	1.822	30
45	5.895	1.119	6.877	1.306	7.860	1.492	8.842	1.679	9.825	1.865	15
11 0	5.890	1.145	6.871	1.336	7.853	1.526	8.835	1.717	9.816	1.908	79 0
15	5.885	1.171	6.866	1.366	7.846	1.561	8.827	1.756	9.808	1.951	45
30	5.880	1.196	6.859	1.396	7.839	1.595	8.819	1.794	9.799	1.994	30
45	5.874	1.222	6.853	1.425	7.832	1.629	8.811	1.833	9.791	2.036	15
12 0	5.869	1.247	6.847	1.455	7.825	1.663	8.803	1.871	9.782	2.079	78 0
15	5.863	1.273	6.841	1.485	7.818	1.697	8.795	1.910	9.772	2.122	45
30	5.858	1.299	6.834	1.515	7.810	1.732	8.787	1.948	9.763	2.164	30
45	5.852	1.324	6.827	1.545	7.803	1.766	8.778	1.986	9.753	2.207	15
13 0	5.846	1.350	6.821	1.575	7.795	1.800	8.769	2.025	9.744	2.250	77 0
15	5.840	1.375	6.814	1.604	7.787	1.834	8.760	2.063	9.734	2.292	45
30	5.834	1.401	6.807	1.634	7.779	1.868	8.751	2.101	9.724	2.335	30
45	5.828	1.426	6.799	1.664	7.771	1.902	8.742	2.139	9.713	2.377	15
14 0	5.822	1.452	6.792	1.693	7.762	1.935	8.733	2.177	9.703	2.419	76 0
15	5.815	1.477	6.785	1.723	7.754	1.969	8.723	2.215	9.692	2.462	45
30	5.809	1.502	6.777	1.753	7.745	2.003	8.713	2.253	9.682	2.504	30
45	5.802	1.528	6.769	1.782	7.736	2.037	8.703	2.291	9.671	2.546	15
15 0	5.796	1.553	6.761	1.812	7.727	2.071	8.693	2.329	9.659	2.588	75 0
° ′	Dep.	Lat.	Dep.	Lat.	Dep.	Lat.	Dep.	Lat.	Dep.	Lat.	° ′
Bearing.	Distance 6.		Distance 7.		Distance 8.		Distance 9.		Distance 10.		Bearing.

15° — 30°

Bearing.	Distance 1.		Distance 2.		Distance 3.		Distance 4.		Distance 5.		Bearing.
° ′	Lat.	Dep.	Lat.	Dep.	Lat.	Dep.	Lat.	Dep.	Lat.	Dep.	° ′
15 15	0.965	0.263	1.930	0.526	2.894	0.789	3.859	1.052	4.824	1.315	74 45
30	0.964	0.267	1.927	0.534	2.891	0.802	3.855	1.069	4.818	1.336	30
45	0.962	0.271	1.925	0.543	2.887	0.814	3.850	1.086	4.812	1.357	15
16 0	0.961	0.276	1.923	0.551	2.884	0.827	3.845	1.103	4.806	1.378	74 0
15	0.960	0.280	1.920	0.560	2.880	0.839	3.840	1.119	4.800	1.399	45
30	0.959	0.284	1.918	0.568	2.876	0.852	3.835	1.136	4.794	1.420	30
45	0.958	0.288	1.915	0.576	2.873	0.865	3.830	1.153	4.788	1.441	15
17 0	0.956	0.292	1.913	0.585	2.869	0.877	3.825	1.169	4.782	1.462	73 0
15	0.955	0.297	1.910	0.593	2.865	0.890	3.820	1.186	4.775	1.483	45
30	0.954	0.301	1.907	0.601	2.861	0.902	3.815	1.203	4.769	1.504	30
45	0.952	0.305	1.905	0.610	2.857	0.915	3.810	1.220	4.762	1.524	15
18 0	0.951	0.309	1.902	0.618	2.853	0.927	3.804	1.236	4.755	1.545	72 0
15	0.950	0.313	1.899	0.626	2.849	0.939	3.799	1.253	4.748	1.566	45
30	0.948	0.317	1.897	0.635	2.845	0.952	3.793	1.269	4.742	1.587	30
45	0.947	0.321	1.894	0.643	2.841	0.964	3.788	1.286	4.735	1.607	15
19 0	0.946	0.326	1.891	0.651	2.837	0.977	3.782	1.302	4.728	1.628	71 0
15	0.944	0.330	1.888	0.659	2.832	0.989	3.776	1.319	4.720	1.648	45
30	0.943	0.334	1.885	0.668	2.828	1.001	3.771	1.335	4.713	1.669	30
45	0.941	0.338	1.882	0.676	2.824	1.014	3.765	1.352	4.706	1.690	15
20 0	0.940	0.342	1.879	0.684	2.819	1.026	3.759	1.368	4.698	1.710	70 0
15	0.938	0.346	1.876	0.692	2.815	1.038	3.753	1.384	4.691	1.731	45
30	0.937	0.350	1.873	0.700	2.810	1.051	3.747	1.401	4.683	1.751	30
45	0.935	0.354	1.870	0.709	2.805	1.063	3.741	1.417	4.676	1.771	15
21 0	0.934	0.358	1.867	0.717	2.801	1.075	3.734	1.433	4.668	1.792	69 0
15	0.932	0.362	1.864	0.725	2.796	1.087	3.728	1.450	4.660	1.812	45
30	0.930	0.367	1.861	0.733	2.791	1.100	3.722	1.466	4.652	1.833	30
45	0.929	0.371	1.858	0.741	2.786	1.112	3.715	1.482	4.644	1.853	15
22 0	0.927	0.375	1.854	0.749	2.782	1.124	3.709	1.498	4.636	1.873	68 0
15	0.926	0.379	1.851	0.757	2.777	1.136	3.702	1.515	4.628	1.893	45
30	0.924	0.383	1.848	0.765	2.772	1.148	3.696	1.531	4.619	1.913	30
45	0.922	0.387	1.844	0.773	2.767	1.160	3.689	1.547	4.611	1.934	15
23 0	0.921	0.391	1.841	0.781	2.762	1.172	3.682	1.563	4.603	1.954	67 0
15	0.919	0.395	1.838	0.789	2.756	1.184	3.675	1.579	4.594	1.974	45
30	0.917	0.399	1.834	0.797	2.751	1.196	3.668	1.595	4.585	1.994	30
45	0.915	0.403	1.831	0.805	2.746	1.208	3.661	1.611	4.577	2.014	15
24 0	0.914	0.407	1.827	0.813	2.741	1.220	3.654	1.627	4.568	2.034	66 0
15	0.912	0.411	1.824	0.821	2.735	1.232	3.647	1.643	4.559	2.054	45
30	0.910	0.415	1.820	0.829	2.730	1.244	3.640	1.659	4.550	2.073	30
45	0.908	0.419	1.816	0.837	2.724	1.256	3.633	1.675	4.541	2.093	15
25 0	0.906	0.423	1.813	0.845	2.719	1.268	3.625	1.690	4.532	2.113	65 0
15	0.904	0.427	1.809	0.853	2.713	1.280	3.618	1.706	4.522	2.133	45
30	0.903	0.431	1.805	0.861	2.708	1.292	3.610	1.722	4.513	2.153	30
45	0.901	0.434	1.801	0.869	2.702	1.303	3.603	1.738	4.503	2.172	15
26 0	0.899	0.438	1.798	0.877	2.696	1.315	3.595	1.753	4.494	2.192	64 0
15	0.897	0.442	1.794	0.885	2.691	1.327	3.587	1.769	4.484	2.211	45
30	0.895	0.446	1.790	0.892	2.685	1.339	3.580	1.785	4.475	2.231	30
45	0.893	0.450	1.786	0.900	2.679	1.350	3.572	1.800	4.465	2.250	15
27 0	0.891	0.454	1.782	0.908	2.673	1.362	3.564	1.816	4.455	2.270	63 0
15	0.889	0.458	1.778	0.916	2.667	1.374	3.556	1.831	4.445	2.289	45
30	0.887	0.462	1.774	0.923	2.661	1.385	3.548	1.847	4.435	2.309	30
45	0.885	0.466	1.770	0.931	2.655	1.397	3.540	1.862	4.425	2.328	15
28 0	0.883	0.469	1.766	0.939	2.649	1.408	3.532	1.878	4.415	2.347	62 0
15	0.881	0.473	1.762	0.947	2.643	1.420	3.524	1.893	4.404	2.367	45
30	0.879	0.477	1.758	0.954	2.636	1.431	3.515	1.909	4.394	2.386	30
45	0.877	0.481	1.753	0.962	2.630	1.443	3.507	1.924	4.384	2.405	15
29 0	0.875	0.485	1.749	0.970	2.624	1.454	3.498	1.939	4.373	2.424	61 0
15	0.872	0.489	1.745	0.977	2.617	1.466	3.490	1.954	4.362	2.443	45
30	0.870	0.492	1.741	0.985	2.611	1.477	3.481	1.970	4.352	2.462	30
45	0.868	0.496	1.736	0.992	2.605	1.489	3.473	1.985	4.341	2.481	15
30 0	0.866	0.500	1.732	1.000	2.598	1.500	3.464	2.000	4.330	2.500	60 0
° ′	Dep.	Lat.	Dep.	Lat.	Dep.	Lat.	Dep.	Lat.	Dep.	Lat.	° ′
Bearing.	Distance 1.		Distance 2.		Distance 3.		Distance 4.		Distance 5.		Bearing.

60° — 75°

Bearing.	Distance 6.		Distance 7.		Distance 8.		Distance 9.		Distance 10.		Bearing.
° ′	Lat.	Dep.	Lat.	Dep.	Lat.	Dep.	Lat.	Dep.	Lat.	Dep.	° ′
15 15	5.789	1.578	6.754	1.841	7.718	2.104	8.683	2.367	9.648	2.630	**74** 45
30	5.782	1.603	6.745	1.871	7.709	2.138	8.673	2.405	9.636	2.672	30
45	5.775	1.629	6.737	1.900	7.700	2.172	8.662	2.443	9.625	2.714	15
16 0	5.768	1.654	6.729	1.929	7.690	2.205	8.651	2.481	9.613	2.756	**74** 0
15	5.760	1.679	6.720	1.959	7.680	2.239	8.640	2.518	9.601	2.798	45
30	5.753	1.704	6.712	1.988	7.671	2.272	8.629	2.556	9.588	2.840	30
45	5.745	1.729	6.703	2.017	7.661	2.306	8.618	2.594	9.576	2.882	15
17 0	5.738	1.754	6.694	2.047	7.650	2.339	8.607	2.631	9.563	2.924	**73** 0
15	5.730	1.779	6.685	2.076	7.640	2.372	8.595	2.669	9.550	2.965	45
30	5.722	1.804	6.676	2.105	7.630	2.406	8.583	2.706	9.537	3.007	30
45	5.714	1.829	6.667	2.134	7.619	2.439	8.572	2.744	9.524	3.049	15
18 0	5.706	1.854	6.657	2.163	7.608	2.472	8.560	2.781	9.511	3.090	**72** 0
15	5.698	1.879	6.648	2.192	7.598	2.505	8.547	2.818	9.497	3.132	45
30	5.690	1.904	6.638	2.221	7.587	2.538	8.535	2.856	9.483	3.173	30
45	5.682	1.929	6.629	2.250	7.575	2.572	8.522	2.893	9.469	3.214	15
19 0	5.673	1.953	6.619	2.279	7.564	2.605	8.510	2.930	9.455	3.256	**71** 0
15	5.665	1.978	6.609	2.308	7.553	2.638	8.497	2.967	9.441	3.297	45
30	5.656	2.003	6.598	2.337	7.541	2.670	8.484	3.004	9.426	3.338	30
45	5.647	2.028	6.588	2.365	7.529	2.703	8.471	3.041	9.412	3.379	15
20 0	5.638	2.052	6.578	2.394	7.518	2.736	8.457	3.078	9.397	3.420	**70** 0
15	5.629	2.077	6.567	2.423	7.506	2.769	8.444	3.115	9.382	3.461	45
30	5.620	2.101	6.557	2.451	7.493	2.802	8.430	3.152	9.367	3.502	30
45	5.611	2.126	6.546	2.480	7.481	2.834	8.416	3.189	9.351	3.543	15
21 0	5.601	2.150	6.535	2.509	7.469	2.867	8.402	3.225	9.336	3.584	**69** 0
15	5.592	2.175	6.524	2.537	7.456	2.900	8.388	3.262	9.320	3.624	45
30	5.582	2.199	6.513	2.566	7.443	2.932	8.374	3.299	9.304	3.665	30
45	5.573	2.223	6.502	2.594	7.430	2.964	8.359	3.335	9.288	3.706	15
22 0	5.563	2.248	6.490	2.622	7.417	2.997	8.345	3.371	9.272	3.746	**68** 0
15	5.553	2.272	6.479	2.651	7.404	3.029	8.330	3.408	9.255	3.787	45
30	5.543	2.296	6.467	2.679	7.391	3.061	8.315	3.444	9.239	3.827	30
45	5.533	2.320	6.455	2.707	7.378	3.094	8.300	3.480	9.222	3.867	15
23 0	5.523	2.344	6.444	2.735	7.364	3.126	8.285	3.517	9.205	3.907	**67** 0
15	5.513	2.368	6.432	2.763	7.350	3.158	8.269	3.553	9.188	3.947	45
30	5.502	2.392	6.419	2.791	7.336	3.190	8.254	3.589	9.171	3.988	30
45	5.492	2.416	6.407	2.819	7.322	3.222	8.238	3.625	9.153	4.028	15
24 0	5.481	2.440	6.395	2.847	7.308	3.254	8.222	3.661	9.136	4.067	**66** 0
15	5.471	2.464	6.382	2.875	7.294	3.286	8.206	3.696	9.118	4.107	45
30	5.460	2.488	6.370	2.903	7.280	3.318	8.190	3.732	9.100	4.147	30
45	5.449	2.512	6.357	2.931	7.265	3.349	8.173	3.768	9.081	4.187	15
25 0	5.438	2.536	6.344	2.958	7.250	3.381	8.157	3.804	9.063	4.226	**65** 0
15	5.427	2.559	6.331	2.986	7.236	3.413	8.140	3.839	9.045	4.266	45
30	5.416	2.583	6.318	3.014	7.221	3.444	8.123	3.875	9.026	4.305	30
45	5.404	2.607	6.305	3.041	7.206	3.476	8.106	3.910	9.007	4.345	15
26 0	5.393	2.630	6.292	3.069	7.190	3.507	8.089	3.945	8.988	4.384	**64** 0
15	5.381	2.654	6.278	3.096	7.175	3.538	8.072	3.981	8.969	4.423	45
30	5.370	2.677	6.265	3.123	7.160	3.570	8.054	4.016	8.949	4.462	30
45	5.358	2.701	6.251	3.151	7.144	3.601	8.037	4.051	8.930	4.501	15
27 0	5.346	2.724	6.237	3.178	7.128	3.632	8.019	4.086	8.910	4.540	**63** 0
15	5.334	2.747	6.223	3.205	7.112	3.663	8.001	4.121	8.890	4.579	45
30	5.322	2.770	6.209	3.232	7.096	3.694	7.983	4.156	8.870	4.618	30
45	5.310	2.794	6.195	3.259	7.080	3.725	7.965	4.190	8.850	4.656	15
28 0	5.298	2.817	6.181	3.286	7.064	3.756	7.947	4.225	8.829	4.695	**62** 0
15	5.285	2.840	6.166	3.313	7.047	3.787	7.928	4.260	8.809	4.733	45
30	5.273	2.863	6.152	3.340	7.031	3.817	7.909	4.294	8.788	4.772	30
45	5.260	2.886	6.137	3.367	7.014	3.848	7.891	4.329	8.767	4.810	15
29 0	5.248	2.909	6.122	3.394	6.997	3.878	7.872	4.363	8.746	4.848	**61** 0
15	5.235	2.932	6.107	3.420	6.980	3.909	7.852	4.398	8.725	4.886	45
30	5.222	2.955	6.093	3.447	6.963	3.939	7.833	4.432	8.704	4.924	30
45	5.209	2.977	6.077	3.474	6.946	3.970	7.814	4.466	8.682	4.962	15
30 0	5.196	3.000	6.062	3.500	6.928	4.000	7.794	4.500	8.660	5.000	**60** 0
° ′	Dep.	Lat.	Dep.	Lat.	Dep.	Lat.	Dep.	Lat.	Dep.	Lat.	° ′
Bearing.	Distance 6.		Distance 7.		Distance 8.		Distance 9.		Distance 10.		Bearing.

Bearing.	Distance 1.		Distance 2.		Distance 3.		Distance 4.		Distance 5.		Bearing.
° ′	Lat.	Dep.	Lat.	Dep.	Lat.	Dep.	Lat.	Dep.	Lat.	Dep.	° ′
30 15	0.864	0.504	1.728	1.008	2.592	1.511	3.455	2.015	4.319	2.519	59 45
30	0.862	0.508	1.723	1.015	2.585	1.523	3.447	2.030	4.308	2.538	30
45	0.859	0.511	1.719	1.023	2.578	1.534	3.438	2.045	4.297	2.556	15
31 0	0.857	0.515	1.714	1.030	2.572	1.545	3.429	2.060	4.286	2.575	59 0
15	0.855	0.519	1.710	1.038	2.565	1.556	3.420	2.075	4.275	2.594	45
30	0.853	0.522	1.705	1.045	2.558	1.567	3.411	2.090	4.263	2.612	30
45	0.850	0.526	1.701	1.052	2.551	1.579	3.401	2.105	4.252	2.631	15
32 0	0.848	0.530	1.696	1.060	2.544	1.590	3.392	2.120	4.240	2.650	58 0
15	0.846	0.534	1.691	1.067	2.537	1.601	3.383	2.134	4.229	2.668	45
30	0.843	0.537	1.687	1.075	2.530	1.612	3.374	2.149	4.217	2.686	30
45	0.841	0.541	1.682	1.082	2.523	1.623	3.364	2.164	4.205	2.705	15
33 0	0.839	0.545	1.677	1.089	2.516	1.634	3.355	2.179	4.193	2.723	57 0
15	0.836	0.548	1.673	1.097	2.509	1.645	3.345	2.193	4.181	2.741	45
30	0.834	0.552	1.668	1.104	2.502	1.656	3.336	2.208	4.169	2.760	30
45	0.831	0.556	1.663	1.111	2.494	1.667	3.326	2.222	4.157	2.778	15
34 0	0.829	0.559	1.658	1.118	2.487	1.678	3.316	2.237	4.145	2.796	56 0
15	0.827	0.563	1.653	1.126	2.480	1.688	3.306	2.251	4.133	2.814	45
30	0.824	0.566	1.648	1.133	2.472	1.699	3.297	2.266	4.121	2.832	30
45	0.822	0.570	1.643	1.140	2.465	1.710	3.287	2.280	4.108	2.850	15
35 0	0.819	0.574	1.638	1.147	2.457	1.721	3.277	2.294	4.096	2.868	55 0
15	0.817	0.577	1.633	1.154	2.450	1.731	3.267	2.309	4.083	2.886	45
30	0.814	0.581	1.628	1.161	2.442	1.742	3.257	2.323	4.071	2.904	30
45	0.812	0.584	1.623	1.168	2.435	1.753	3.246	2.337	4.058	2.921	15
36 0	0.809	0.588	1.618	1.176	2.427	1.763	3.236	2.351	4.045	2.939	54 0
15	0.806	0.591	1.613	1.183	2.419	1.774	3.226	2.365	4.032	2.957	45
30	0.804	0.595	1.608	1.190	2.412	1.784	3.215	2.379	4.019	2.974	30
45	0.801	0.598	1.603	1.197	2.404	1.795	3.205	2.393	4.006	2.992	15
37 0	0.799	0.602	1.597	1.204	2.396	1.805	3.195	2.407	3.993	3.009	53 0
15	0.796	0.605	1.592	1.211	2.388	1.816	3.184	2.421	3.980	3.026	45
30	0.793	0.609	1.587	1.218	2.380	1.826	3.173	2.435	3.967	3.044	30
45	0.791	0.612	1.581	1.224	2.372	1.837	3.163	2.449	3.953	3.061	15
38 0	0.788	0.616	1.576	1.231	2.364	1.847	3.152	2.463	3.940	3.078	52 0
15	0.785	0.619	1.571	1.238	2.356	1.857	3.141	2.476	3.927	3.095	45
30	0.783	0.623	1.565	1.245	2.348	1.868	3.130	2.490	3.913	3.113	30
45	0.780	0.626	1.560	1.252	2.340	1.878	3.120	2.504	3.899	3.130	15
39 0	0.777	0.629	1.554	1.259	2.331	1.888	3.109	2.517	3.886	3.147	51 0
15	0.774	0.633	1.549	1.265	2.323	1.898	3.098	2.531	3.872	3.164	45
30	0.772	0.636	1.543	1.272	2.315	1.908	3.086	2.544	3.858	3.180	30
45	0.769	0.639	1.538	1.279	2.307	1.918	3.075	2.558	3.844	3.197	15
40 0	0.766	0.643	1.532	1.286	2.298	1.928	3.064	2.571	3.830	3.214	50 0
15	0.763	0.646	1.526	1.292	2.290	1.938	3.053	2.584	3.816	3.231	45
30	0.760	0.649	1.521	1.299	2.281	1.948	3.042	2.598	3.802	3.247	30
45	0.758	0.653	1.515	1.306	2.273	1.958	3.030	2.611	3.788	3.264	15
41 0	0.755	0.656	1.509	1.312	2.264	1.968	3.019	2.624	3.774	3.280	49 0
15	0.752	0.659	1.504	1.319	2.256	1.978	3.007	2.637	3.759	3.297	45
30	0.749	0.663	1.498	1.325	2.247	1.988	2.996	2.650	3.745	3.313	30
45	0.746	0.666	1.492	1.332	2.238	1.998	2.984	2.664	3.730	3.329	15
42 0	0.743	0.669	1.486	1.338	2.229	2.007	2.973	2.677	3.716	3.346	48 0
15	0.740	0.672	1.480	1.345	2.221	2.017	2.961	2.689	3.701	3.362	45
30	0.737	0.676	1.475	1.351	2.212	2.027	2.949	2.702	3.686	3.378	30
45	0.734	0.679	1.469	1.358	2.203	2.036	2.937	2.715	3.672	3.394	15
43 0	0.731	0.682	1.463	1.364	2.194	2.046	2.925	2.728	3.657	3.410	47 0
15	0.728	0.685	1.457	1.370	2.185	2.056	2.913	2.741	3.642	3.426	45
30	0.725	0.688	1.451	1.377	2.176	2.065	2.901	2.753	3.627	3.442	30
45	0.722	0.692	1.445	1.383	2.167	2.075	2.889	2.766	3.612	3.458	15
44 0	0.719	0.695	1.439	1.389	2.158	2.084	2.877	2.779	3.597	3.473	46 0
15	0.716	0.698	1.433	1.396	2.149	2.093	2.865	2.791	3.582	3.489	45
30	0.713	0.701	1.427	1.402	2.140	2.103	2.853	2.804	3.566	3.505	30
45	0.710	0.704	1.420	1.408	2.131	2.112	2.841	2.816	3.551	3.520	15
45 0	0.707	0.707	1.414	1.414	2.121	2.121	2.828	2.828	3.536	3.536	45 0
° ′	Dep.	Lat.	Dep.	Lat.	Dep.	Lat.	Dep.	Lat.	Dep.	Lat.	° ′
Bearing.	Distance 1.		Distance 2.		Distance 3.		Distance 4.		Distance 5.		Bearing.

Bearing	Distance 6.		Distance 7.		Distance 8.		Distance 9.		Distance 10.		Bearing
° ′	Lat.	Dep.	Lat.	Dep.	Lat.	Dep.	Lat.	Dep.	Lat.	Dep.	° ′
30 15	5.183	3.023	6.047	3.526	6.911	4.030	7.775	4.534	8.638	5.038	**59** 45
30	5.170	3.045	6.031	3.553	6.893	4.060	7.755	4.568	8.616	5.075	30
45	5.156	3.068	6.016	3.579	6.875	4.090	7.735	4.602	8.594	5.113	15
31 0	5.143	3.090	6.000	3.605	6.857	4.120	7.715	4.635	8.572	5.150	**59** 0
15	5.129	3.113	5.984	3.631	6.839	4.150	7.694	4.669	8.549	5.188	45
30	5.116	3.135	5.968	3.657	6.821	4.180	7.674	4.702	8.526	5.225	30
45	5.102	3.157	5.952	3.683	6.803	4.210	7.653	4.736	8.504	5.262	15
32 0	5.088	3.180	5.936	3.709	6.784	4.239	7.632	4.769	8.481	5.299	**58** 0
15	5.074	3.202	5.920	3.735	6.766	4.269	7.612	4.802	8.457	5.336	45
30	5.060	3.224	5.904	3.761	6.747	4.298	7.591	4.836	8.434	5.373	30
45	5.046	3.246	5.887	3.787	6.728	4.328	7.569	4.869	8.410	5.410	15
33 0	5.032	3.268	5.871	3.812	6.709	4.357	7.548	4.902	8.387	5.446	**57** 0
15	5.018	3.290	5.854	3.838	6.690	4.386	7.527	4.935	8.363	5.483	45
30	5.003	3.312	5.837	3.864	6.671	4.416	7.505	4.967	8.339	5.519	30
45	4.989	3.333	5.820	3.889	6.652	4.445	7.483	5.000	8.315	5.556	15
34 0	4.974	3.355	5.803	3.914	6.632	4.474	7.461	5.033	8.290	5.592	**56** 0
15	4.960	3.377	5.786	3.940	6.613	4.502	7.439	5.065	8.266	5.628	45
30	4.945	3.398	5.769	3.965	6.593	4.531	7.417	5.098	8.241	5.664	30
45	4.930	3.420	5.752	3.990	6.573	4.560	7.395	5.130	8.217	5.700	15
35 0	4.915	3.441	5.734	4.015	6.553	4.589	7.372	5.162	8.192	5.736	**55** 0
15	4.900	3.463	5.716	4.040	6.533	4.617	7.350	5.194	8.166	5.772	45
30	4.885	3.484	5.699	4.065	6.513	4.646	7.327	5.226	8.141	5.807	30
45	4.869	3.505	5.681	4.090	6.493	4.674	7.304	5.258	8.116	5.843	15
36 0	4.854	3.527	5.663	4.115	6.472	4.702	7.281	5.290	8.090	5.878	**54** 0
15	4.839	3.548	5.645	4.139	6.452	4.730	7.258	5.322	8.064	5.913	45
30	4.823	3.569	5.627	4.164	6.431	4.759	7.235	5.353	8.039	5.948	30
45	4.808	3.590	5.609	4.188	6.410	4.787	7.211	5.385	8.013	5.983	15
37 0	4.792	3.611	5.590	4.213	6.389	4.815	7.188	5.416	7.986	6.018	**53** 0
15	4.776	3.632	5.572	4.237	6.368	4.842	7.164	5.448	7.960	6.053	45
30	4.760	3.653	5.554	4.261	6.347	4.870	7.140	5.479	7.934	6.088	30
45	4.744	3.673	5.535	4.286	6.326	4.898	7.116	5.510	7.907	6.122	15
38 0	4.728	3.694	5.516	4.310	6.304	4.925	7.092	5.541	7.880	6.157	**52** 0
15	4.712	3.715	5.497	4.334	6.283	4.953	7.068	5.572	7.853	6.191	45
30	4.696	3.735	5.478	4.358	6.261	4.980	7.043	5.603	7.826	6.225	30
45	4.679	3.756	5.459	4.381	6.239	5.007	7.019	5.633	7.799	6.259	15
39 0	4.663	3.776	5.440	4.405	6.217	5.035	6.994	5.664	7.772	6.293	**51** 0
15	4.646	3.796	5.421	4.429	6.195	5.062	6.970	5.694	7.744	6.327	45
30	4.630	3.816	5.401	4.453	6.173	5.089	6.945	5.725	7.716	6.361	30
45	4.613	3.837	5.382	4.476	6.151	5.116	6.920	5.755	7.688	6.394	15
40 0	4.596	3.857	5.362	4.500	6.128	5.142	6.894	5.785	7.660	6.428	**50** 0
15	4.579	3.877	5.343	4.523	6.106	5.169	6.869	5.815	7.632	6.461	45
30	4.562	3.897	5.323	4.546	6.083	5.196	6.844	5.845	7.604	6.495	30
45	4.545	3.917	5.303	4.569	6.061	5.222	6.818	5.875	7.576	6.528	15
41 0	4.528	3.936	5.283	4.592	6.038	5.248	6.792	5.905	7.547	6.561	**49** 0
15	4.511	3.956	5.263	4.615	6.015	5.275	6.767	5.934	7.518	6.594	45
30	4.494	3.976	5.243	4.638	5.992	5.301	6.741	5.964	7.490	6.626	30
45	4.476	3.995	5.222	4.661	5.968	5.327	6.715	5.993	7.461	6.659	15
42 0	4.459	4.015	5.202	4.684	5.945	5.353	6.688	6.022	7.431	6.691	**48** 0
15	4.441	4.034	5.182	4.707	5.922	5.379	6.662	6.051	7.402	6.724	45
30	4.424	4.054	5.161	4.729	5.898	5.405	6.635	6.080	7.373	6.756	30
45	4.406	4.073	5.140	4.752	5.875	5.430	6.609	6.109	7.343	6.788	15
43 0	4.388	4.092	5.119	4.774	5.851	5.456	6.582	6.138	7.314	6.820	**47** 0
15	4.370	4.111	5.099	4.796	5.827	5.481	6.555	6.167	7.284	6.852	45
30	4.352	4.130	5.078	4.818	5.803	5.507	6.528	6.195	7.254	6.884	30
45	4.334	4.149	5.057	4.841	5.779	5.532	6.501	6.224	7.224	6.915	15
44 0	4.316	4.168	5.035	4.863	5.755	5.557	6.474	6.252	7.193	6.947	**46** 0
15	4.298	4.187	5.014	4.885	5.730	5.582	6.447	6.280	7.163	6.978	45
30	4.280	4.206	4.993	4.906	5.706	5.607	6.419	6.308	7.133	7.009	30
45	4.261	4.224	4.971	4.928	5.681	5.632	6.392	6.336	7.102	7.040	15
45 0	4.243	4.243	4.950	4.950	5.657	5.657	6.364	6.364	7.071	7.071	**45** 0
° ′	Dep.	Lat.	Dep.	Lat.	Dep.	Lat.	Dep.	Lat.	Dep.	Lat.	° ′
Bearing	Distance 6.		Distance 7.		Distance 8.		Distance 9.		Distance 10.		Bearing

SURVEYING

AND

TRAVERSE TABLE

BY

G. A. WENTWORTH, A.M.

AUTHOR OF A SERIES OF TEXT-BOOKS IN MATHEMATICS

REVISED EDITION

BOSTON, U.S.A., AND LONDON

GINN & COMPANY, PUBLISHERS

1896